D1588767

530 022 14 9

MARIA HATZISTEFANIS

HOW TO
MAKE IT HAPPEN

TURNING FAILURE INTO SUCCESS

EBURY
PRESS

1 3 5 7 9 10 8 6 4 2

Published in 2020 by Ebury Press, an imprint of Ebury Publishing,
20 Vauxhall Bridge Road,
London SW1V 2SA

Ebury Press is part of the Penguin Random House group of companies
whose addresses can be found at global.penguinrandomhouse.com

Copyright © Maria Hatzistefanis 2020

Maria Hatzistefanis has asserted her right to be identified as the author
of this Work in accordance with the Copyright, Designs and
Patents Act 1988

This edition published by Ebury Press in 2020

www.penguin.co.uk

A CIP catalogue record for this book is available from the British Library

ISBN 9781529105933

Typeset in 11/13 pt Avenir LT Std
by Integra Software Services Pvt. Ltd, Pondicherry

Printed and bound in Great Britain by Clays Ltd, Elcograf S.p.A.

Penguin Random House is committed to a sustainable
future for our business, our readers and our planet.
This book is made from Forest Stewardship Council®
certified paper.

To everyone who ever rejected me, a big thank you for making me the person I am today

Contents

Introduction: How I made it happen

No one is more shocked than I am. I'm a bestselling author, I'm @MrsRodial with over a million followers, I'm the CEO of an international beauty brand, the *Sunday Times's Style* magazine says I'm worth over £100 million, after 18-plus years I'm an 'Overnight Success' and I've just finished my second book ... the one you are holding. I am rewriting the introduction because as of right now all of the above means nothing ... in fact it's all gone horribly, horribly wrong.

Deep breath. Just say it. I'm not worth £100 million. Far from it. In fact, as I write this I'm in danger of going completely broke. Things are bad. Really bad.

Why am I telling you this? God knows I've been trying to keep a lid on it for a while, so why you, why now? It seems I'm not what you think I am, so why should you listen to anything I have to say about business or success now?

You should listen because I am not a quitter and, shocking as this whole situation is to me, I know I will get through this. The lessons I learn will make me stronger. This is a mountain to climb for sure, but it's just another mountain. I'll reach the top, I'll conquer it. I have faith.

That's what this whole book is about. It's about believing you can do it – believing you can make it happen. As my business problems swirled around me I had put this book on the back burner, but then I came to realise that everything I needed to know and use to get through these problems I had just written down right here, handily separated into chapters. However, the 'fun' intro I'd written didn't sit right any more: name-dropping tales of jet-setting and Fashion Week parties weren't working for me given the current situation. I took a deep breath and decided to rewrite this introduction, and tell you that this is what life and business are really like. There is failure, there is rejection, there is pain. This book gives you the naked truth about how I face up to life and business, and how these lessons will help to get me up that mountain. I hope they help you too.

OK, I've been vague so far, but I guess you'd like to know what actually happened.

Despite 20 years in the business I'm still new to this ... I've never run a company that's been going for 20 years before! It was my fault: I just couldn't stop saying 'yes'. Yes to this, yes to that. I was going with my gut ... these were great opportunities. The stores will give us more space for more product, orders will be huge, we'll double the business ... suddenly we had 60 product launches all happening over the course of 120 days. That's one product launch every two days! No one was properly checking how all this would work in terms of cash flow, but we have always pushed the boundaries and danced on the edge a little. This is another bold move, sure, but it will all be a grand success. Won't it?

It all comes suddenly into sharp focus when my financial controller calls for an urgent meeting. She doesn't mess about, she just tells me straight. We are about to go £2 million under and only have an overdraft of £600,000. For a company that is turning over tens of millions and has always been profitable, this is shocking. I am numbed. A cold wave washes over me as I shiver and blink out of a stunned daze and back into the room. OMG. How are we going to pay salaries, suppliers ... anybody? Am I going to be bankrupt, am I going to get sued, am I going down? Btw, what colour are the jumpsuits in debtors' prison? Something hideous no doubt. OK, snap out of it, this is serious.

I immediately call the bank to try to get a bigger overdraft. They suggest they might be able to squeeze me in for lunch in about two weeks? TWO WEEKS!?!? This is a life or death situation over here! I don't have two weeks! OK, can I send them a detailed plan of how we will get out of the red? Action stations! For 48 hours myself and a small, trusted team worked on the plan ... no sleep, lots of coffee, lots of numbers ... it looks good. This will work. Send to the bank.

After an agonising wait they come back to me ... no solutions, just more questions! Arrgh! My bank is really letting me down. Meanwhile, days have passed and the situation has got worse. My phone is red hot. I have suppliers, landlords, salaries all overdue. We are behind on Every. Single. Payment.

Time for drastic action. First I call my suppliers and work out a payment plan. These are the most difficult, humbling calls I have ever had to make ... but I have great suppliers and they (mostly) agree to the terms to give me some time. I am in need of a therapist, a coach and multiple meditations to get through the day.

Next I cut down all the office budgets. Staffing, PR events, digital, office biscuits – all slashed. My staff are confused, obviously, and it occurs to me that I still haven't told them. I can't, it's just too hard. We'll be fine ... they'll never know. Just a few more days, but those days are long ... and I want to keep this contained. Loose Lips Sink Ships.

Now I'm taking control of stock orders, and stopping or delaying as many things as I can to reduce future payments.

We have to go 'out of stock' on several lines. There is no other way. My sales teams are screaming at me to re-stock but I'm telling them to drive sales, we need new business to keep going. I'm attacking this from every angle I can and my teams are getting really pissed off and confused, but they are not the ones having sleepless nights. I don't – I can't – care what they think or say. I have to do what I can to save my business.

Finally, the bank calls. They will increase my overdraft to £1 million for one month. Great news … but with a catch. They want personal guarantees. Meaning if I don't repay the million at the end of the month they will take my personal possessions. I'll be homeless, my kids won't have a school to go to, I'll have nothing. Being an entrepreneur is not for the faint at heart. I feel like I have been hit by a car.

Did it work? Am I homeless? Do the debtors' prison jumpsuits suit my skin tone?

Well, I'm not homeless yet. It did work, I did pay back the overdraft and am still in business. But it was a hard lesson … and it's not over yet. We are still paying back suppliers, catching up on debts, keeping a close eye on the office biscuit budget. I am still learning, just the same as I was when I started out.

Now as then, I realised that I just had to have faith. I had to have faith I could get through this, that I would find the answers, that it would all be all right. Just as 20 years ago I had to have faith that this crazy business idea would work. Even at the darkest times I had the faith that I could Make It Happen.

In the middle of all of this stress and panic, when I was still putting on a 'business as usual' face, one of the things I had to do was a speak at a conference. Here I was, being touted as an inspirational business woman when I knew the ship was going down in flames underneath me.

At the event, everyone thinks I am in control, but everything is moving around me so quickly. It is not a winning season ... Is this it? Is this a failure too far?

Need to keep calm to give my keynote. Make it on stage. Microphone is live. Spotlight on me. Breathe. Focus. The first question from the floor is: 'You are an entrepreneur, a mum, a public figure. How do you motivate yourself to make it happen?'

Wow. After an overwhelming few weeks, up pops this question. How do I 'make it happen'? Those three words, 'make it happen', hit me like a lightning bolt. If this was a film you'd see the shot of my suddenly frozen face looking directly into the lens ... the camera would zoom in to my right eye, closer and closer, with a huge whooshing sound effect as it seemed to travel through my pupil and into my mind, taking me back, with echoey twinkly music and a soft-focus filter, right back to when I first started.

Those three words loomed large: make it happen. When I started without any experience or background, I would say to myself: make it happen. When I wanted to get my products into stores and no one was taking my calls, I'd say: make it happen. When I wanted to work with a big celebrity who didn't even know we existed, it was always: make it happen. And when I had a family in the middle of all this and had to juggle a thousand things while still driving the business, I would say: JUST make it happen.

This has been one of my trademark expressions. Ever since we were a tiny start-up with three people at my first office, I would say at the end of every meeting: make it happen. I still remember the energy that we all got from thinking big, and while we knew we were the smallest fish in the biggest pond, with our drive, positive energy and hard work, we would make it happen in the end.

And what a journey this has been, with so many 'make it happen' moments. Growing from a backroom at home to a global beauty empire working with celebrities such as Kim Kardashian, Ellie Goulding, Jourdan Dunn. Growing our teams to hundreds of people with hubs in London, New York and LA and stores all over the world. Despite the current situation, I look back and can't believe I achieved the things I achieved with one phrase leading me: make it happen. In fact, when I moved into my first office, I had that very phrase printed in big letters on our boardroom wall to make sure my team and I remember where we started. To remember we can always 'make it happen'.

Time to answer the question … How do I make it happen? That's what I do every day … I've been doing it since the very start.

Well, if you have this book in your hands and have got this far I am guessing you might be interested in hearing my reply. It's pretty simple … same as it has always been. Set your goal, plot your trajectory, then make it happen. This is what I do every day, every month, every year. Have a dream … make it happen. Don't give up, don't be diverted, don't lose faith. Make. It. Happen.

As I am answering the question I realise that, in my head, I am starting to solve the problems and come to terms with these crazy few weeks. I can't wait to get back to the office, get together with my team and marvel at how crazy it's been. We'll laugh about it, someone will say 'you should put that in your next book' and we will get back on with the business of making it happen.

I have always found it fascinating when people think that, after I grew my business to where it is today, it now runs by itself while I swan around at fashion shows or premieres. That I have made my success and just step back and bask in the glory. Well, as you have seen, it turns out that success is not final and failure is not fatal. You would think that if you reach a certain level of success that you have nothing to worry about. I know now that's not quite true. There are always challenges to overcome, there are always fires to extinguish; each one is different, burns at a different rate, needs a different extinguisher to quench it.

When I started, my main worry was whether we would survive another day. Now things have changed, and while I am still thinking about keeping my business profitable and afloat in this very competitive market, the stakes are higher. With new challenges along the way, a lot more is at stake. Bigger accounts, bigger teams. Even a small problem can snowball into a massive issue, particularly if I take my eye off the ball. Things are now more complicated to sort out and the stress is no less. Add to that having to juggle family and work, and it never gets easy.

I want to be clear: this financial crisis was not the first time I had faced failure. I have failed a fair amount in my life. In my twenties I didn't know what I wanted to do with my life. I moved from one country to another trying to find a future for myself. I pivoted from one career to another without a plan. I finally landed what I thought was my dream job and got fired for not being good enough. I started a business, failed to get investment and it took me years to get it off the ground. I got knocked down and had doors slammed in my face again and again. Rejection and failure were my everyday reality. No one believed in me. I didn't have experience, connections or money. No one showed me how things get done – I had to figure it out myself. And I made mistake after mistake. Time after time. And just kept going. Rejection and failure were the best things that happened to me. This is how I developed a thick skin and now I like to think that nothing can faze me. As I say, I 'like' to think that ...

But then there are the times that are absolutely horrible ... like the one I have just described. Where everything that can go wrong does go wrong. There are days when I question myself and my judgement and I often ask myself if I am even supposed to be doing this. I can't say it's easy to get out of a bad day or a bad situation but, having done this for many years and seen how most problems do sort themselves out eventually, either by accident or design, I ultimately think, *It will all be OK in the end, and if it's not OK yet, it's not the end*. Also, I am very much into the 'if one door closes, another better one is about to open' philosophy. You have to think like that and I'd place a sizeable bet that most successful people think the same. Are there times when I work on a goal and work hard on it but I don't get where I want to be? Absolutely! What I do is try to put a positive spin on it: maybe it wasn't meant to be, it's leaving the space for something better to come along ... and invariably it does.

I can't go any further without talking about motivation. Without motivation I could not have dragged myself into the office every day when the business seemed to be going under. If I hadn't stayed motivated it would be a very different story. Without motivation nothing will happen. Nothing! In order to make it happen, whether in life or business, you need to find your motivation. I do wish there was a motivation pill that we could take that would give us everlasting motivation. (Note to self: start working on Rodial motivation pills – NIP+WIN? Make It Fab? Dragon Stamina? OK, some work to do here.) Until I can find the magic formula we are all going to need to find *our own* motivation. And renew it, every single day.

There are days when I wake up and I am on fire. I feel energised, full of positive charge and ready to get out and seize the day. And there are days when I just feel very heavy and wish I had someone to motivate me to get things done and be the best person I can be. It happens to all of us: there are just some days when it's hard to find that inner drive to make it happen.

I've never had a boss or a mentor who would motivate or drive me to achieve my goals. I always had to find it in myself to get going. Over time I developed specific strategies, routines and rituals that help motivate me and drive me to chase my dreams. I want to share these with you so you can motivate yourself to achieve *your* dreams. Whatever background, age or stage in your life you are at, there is always space for motivation to drive you to improve yourself. Whether you want to be the best that you can or need the motivation to keep going or are confused and need some direction to follow your dreams, I hope my book gives you the tools to take control of your life and achieve your goals ... instead of just settling for average and sailing through. It really doesn't take much to be the best that you can be.

I truly believe that everything I have achieved in my life is because of my 'make it happen' attitude. If a potentially great opportunity comes my way I say 'yes' and I figure out how I am going to make it work later. What's the worst that can happen? Yes, I might fail, and I have failed more times than I have succeeded but I dusted myself off, learned from my mistakes and kept on going. The 'make it happen' mindset also helped me think big. There were times when I would think of the craziest idea and the 'make it happen' attitude (reinforced by the three-foot-high letters on my boardroom wall) made me think that everything is possible, as long you hustle and work hard, as hard as you can. And don't get me wrong, sometimes you look back on that hard work and it seems like you just stood still. There are times when I feel I must be working harder than anyone else on this planet, harder than I ever did before and the results are still not there, but the next day, you get up, take your Rodial motivation pill (I really must do this) and start working again. There are no guarantees and no one owes me anything. I need to hustle every step of the way to make it happen ... and success has not changed that. I hustle as much these days as I did when I started. There is always a new goal, there is always a new battle to win.

Success is never straightforward, it takes a few failures to get it right. I almost went from being an Overnight Success to an Overnight Failure but I kept on fighting and turned it around. Oh and by the way ... my first book wasn't really an Overnight Success. It just seemed that way. I worked like crazy to get that thing written, published, promoted and talked about, and after several years of blood, sweat and ink ... voilà, an Overnight Success!

For me success is an ongoing mission and my true passion. And while I am still working through my own journey to success, I feel I have the experience and, following my most recent brush with disaster, have pretty much seen it all, so now I want to share my 'make it happen' philosophy with you. I want to show you how my experiences can help you to think big, to say yes to opportunities and not fear failing. I want you to be driven and motivated and I want you to believe that everything is possible if you believe in yourself. *You can make it happen.*

Fasten your seatbelts and enjoy the *Make It Happen* ride.

With all my love,
Xmaria

1

Slay: How to Get Started

Who do you think is holding you back from achieving your dreams?

We are at times our own worst enemies. We find it very easy to self-doubt and sometimes we give up before we even really try. I am certainly guilty of this. There are times when I waiver, when I start to think that others are more successful than me because, because, because ... I would hear myself coming up with the same old excuses ... oh, it's because of my background ... well if I had their connections ... if my circumstances were the same as theirs, etc., etc. This is natural. We all have a fight-or-flight mode tucked away deep in our brains and sometimes it's just easier to give up, to go where it's safe, to escape the sabre-toothed tiger/ fortnightly accounts meeting. You have to fight this. I had to dream big and follow every single dream of mine and get rid of the noise that told me, and still tries to tell me, I'm not good enough.

I should explain why I just referenced sabre-toothed tigers. Well, as you may have heard, humans (and in fact all creatures) have deep-rooted behaviours and instincts that are born with us. These innate behaviours are the reason cats jump when they see a cucumber because they think it is a snake (if you have never watched this online I urge you to); they are why baby turtles head towards the sea and caterpillars make cocoons; they are why dogs drool when they see food and I drool when I see Ryan Gosling ... it's all just a basic instinct. All of this behaviour has been passed down from ancient ancestry and is hardwired into our brains.

Even though you will never get rid of these innate behaviours, you can override them. You can beat the instinct to play safe, you can fight the desire to hide in your cave ... but it takes extra effort, extra commitment and extra belief, and the example of people who have done it ... which is the main reason I am writing this book.

I was born on a remote island in Greece. We didn't even have a beauty store. I didn't go to a fancy school. I wasn't raised in a major city. I wasn't good enough for my first job and got fired. When I decided to start my own business, as I mentioned, I didn't manage to get investment. I certainly wasn't the prettiest or the loudest so people didn't immediately pay attention to me. I had all the excuses that I needed to quite happily never do anything with myself or my life. But I didn't. I fought my way up and out. I got used to hitting bumps and kept on moving. No one did me any favours. Yes, I have received advice and assistance along the way but, in the end, everything I have done I have done for myself: I have worked hard and I hustled. No one told me how to do it, no one showed me the way. I figured it out myself. I dreamed big and now I am following my dreams.

Against all odds, I built two global brands (Rodial and NIP+FAB). Against all odds, I wrote a book that became a bestseller. Against all odds, I met the most fascinating celebrities in the world. It's not easy and it didn't happen overnight. In my book *How to Be an Overnight Success*, I explain exactly how that single night happened to last 18 years. It wasn't easy and it had its challenges. And yes, there are still moments when I come up with excuses. In fact, it occurs to me that just saying 'against all odds' is a bit of an excuse … it suggests that I got here by fluke, that somehow I played the lottery and won … no skill, no talent, I just happened to fall ass backwards into a barrel of sawdust and emerge with the winning ticket. Erm … I don't think so, babes. (You need to imagine me with my hand on my hip, and my head cocked to one side in a sassy attitude here.) I worked hard, damn hard, every single day to get here … I made this success myself. So when you look back, don't forget it was no fluke, you made this, you got here yourself.

4

But I get that it is sometimes hard to see a way through. We go on Instagram and there are some days when everyone seems to be super successful. They are posting about new deals, new collaborations, winning awards, having the perfect family, wardrobe or holidays. Even their 'fails' are funny and cute and getting 20 million likes. This is tough to take on board when you are having a bad day: here, laid out in gloriously vibrant pixels, is a seemingly never-ending story of glamour and success, while you are living on Super Noodles and it won't stop raining.

Of course, this is just social media. No one is 100 per cent successful, or 100 per cent happy, or 100 per cent beautiful … that's just what they choose to show. (You know that, of course: we are all grown-ups here.) But this is a positive. You should look at these people, companies, celebrities or friends as a motivation for your future million-follower feed. Learn from them. They are achieving great things, but they are not doing anything that you can't match.

Excuses are a way for us to give up before we even try. You want to achieve a certain goal but you are already thinking of five reasons why this won't succeed. We all have an internal mechanism that helps us make the right decisions, either through gut or logic. But we are also naturally risk averse, and by using excuses we are overprotecting ourselves to avoid failure (and sabre-toothed tigers), meaning we don't take action, meaning we will never succeed.

The key to being successful is to have an entrepreneurial attitude. And by that I don't mean that everyone needs or has to start their own business. There are many successful people who have made their mark working for someone else, and many of my personal role models work for companies and lead inspiring and exciting lives. Who doesn't admire the success of Anna Wintour? As the editor

5

of American *Vogue* she is actually an employee of Condé Nast, but not owning her own business does not diminish her success. She is a powerhouse of a woman in an industry that she loves and has achieved the success that anyone would have dreamed of. I think it is a misconception that you can only be successful when you have your own business. I know many unsuccessful people who have their own business. Through the hype of shows such as *Shark Tank* and *Dragons' Den*, having one's own business has been made to look like the only way to be truly happy and successful in work. Of course, for some this is true, but for every successful business owner there are thousands of struggling ones and equally there are a lot of successful people who have carved out amazing careers for themselves working for a company. You can go after success and chase your dreams in any industry and job and lead a happy and fulfilled career and life. There are different goals to achieve, different interests to pursue, and success looks very different to every single one of us. But one thing is for sure – all successful people have a similar mindset.

Over the years, I've had employees come to me and say, 'I want the business to invest in me and put in place a plan for my personal development.' And of course, I want to develop my team and allow them to reach their full potential. But at the same time these comments perplex and exasperate me. When I look back on my career path, I had to figure it all out myself ... and I still am figuring it out, day by day. Always learning, always improving. No one told me what to do, no one put together a development plan for me. I have certainly developed myself over the years but I have taken personal development into my own hands. I read articles, listen to podcasts, watch YouTube videos ... Every day I want to learn something new. Inspiration and life lessons can come from anywhere. So while I keep myself updated on trends in fashion and the beauty industry, and read articles on management, leadership and business practice, I also keep my eye on world affairs, nutritional trends, fitness and yes ... even sport. I take control of my personal development and I don't depend on anyone to do this for me. I want to be in control of my destiny and not ask others to define how I will develop.

And that is the advice I give to those who ask me to help them develop ... I can give you some advice, but the investment has to come from you. And it works. I have a few of my team who have been with me for many years, and who have learned to do exactly that. They figure it out themselves, keep up to speed with the industry, educate themselves and always challenge themselves to be better. I know that they will be successful because they have the right attitude, energy and self-belief that comes with doing it for yourself.

And remember, you are not defined by your job title. Even though companies might make an effort to make everybody sound like they are doing an important job by fancying up their job titles, it really doesn't matter what it says on your card: it's what you do that counts. I've had personal assistants in the past who were running everything for me, from my book tour to my TV shows to representing me at meetings. They could quite happily and easily run the whole company, and probably would have jumped at it if I had offered. By contrast, I've come across people who thought it was a tough day sitting at a desk and booking travel arrangements ... these are the types who ask for the 'personal development plan'. Both types might have the same choices, but the former will choose to run with the opportunities and the latter aren't able to see beyond their job title, and are blind to the possibilities for self-improvement. You can take your job and your life where you want it to be but you need to be open and alive to chance and possibility. Regardless of your title, create the role that you want and make your job your dream.

Having said that, I realise that some bosses are not quite so free thinking and may want you to stay within very rigid boundaries. That may be OK, but if it is not, if you feel tied down or hemmed in then you must move on, change roles, go for the promotion, or leave and find a company that you can grow with. It is all down to you. No one else is going to get you there. People who struggle to achieve success always seem to be waiting for someone else to develop them and motivate them and, while this may happen, wouldn't it feel so much better if you figured it out all by yourself? Wouldn't that make you feel proud?

Remember, if someone else isn't making it happen for you, make it happen for yourself.

I don't know whether people are born naturally motivated or not ... but I do know that it is something that everyone has in them. Motivation is a skill that you can grow over the years. When I was young, social media wasn't a thing and it was hard to find role models. I was thirsty to learn. I was devouring fashion magazines and buying a lot of 'how to ...' books to learn more about my passions (fashion and writing). I didn't have the right connections or go to the right schools to set me up nicely for a good life and a career. I wanted to learn new skills, improve in any way I could, and get inspiration to become someone who makes a difference in the world. Now, I did find my motivation and my passion early, but there is no time limit on this. If you are reading this and saying, 'Ah yes, that's all very well, but I'm in my fifties so it's too late for me,' I refer you back to the beginning of this chapter. *No excuses!*

Almost all the successful people I know have one thing in common: humble beginnings. When you start from the

8

very bottom and have no sense of entitlement, you work harder and you end up being more successful.

It doesn't matter where you are in life. Motivation will help you realise your dream. At the age of 65, Harland Sanders had to sell his small gas station restaurant. It had been quite popular in its heyday ... particularly his chicken recipe ... so much so that people had nicknamed him the 'Colonel' of Fried Chicken. But now, with only $105 a month social security and a chicken recipe to his name, things were looking bleak for a happy retirement. So, to make a bit extra he started selling his chicken door to door. It was very popular and he soon had enough to open his own restaurant, which became a chain, which became a global phenomenon. At the age of 72, Harland 'Colonel' Sanders sold his stake in KFC and was a multi-millionaire.

What motivates me? Outside the typical role models of strong successful women, I also have some more unusual and personal role models that motivate me at times. When I recently had corrective PRK eye surgery I didn't realise that I would have trouble seeing anything for the following week. As usual my diary was packed wall-to-wall and I had committed to being part of a panel discussion on social media at a London conference just a few days after my surgery. I felt great, trouble was I couldn't see anything! What would I do? I am not one to cancel and I never like to let people down, but I was struggling to function. How was I going to get on stage and perform? And then my grandmother came to mind. She is in her nineties, almost blind, and every day she still gets up, walks to the local market to meet her friends and buys her daily shopping. I thought about her and I immediately felt like a wimp! That was the kick in the ass that I needed to go ahead with my plans. Life is never perfect, but that's no excuse.

Despite her age and the physical challenges she has to go through, it is a massive inspiration to know that she perseveres through the pains and downright hassles of old age and yet still has a great energy for life. Every. Single. Day. And so, thinking about my grandmother made me realise I actually had no excuse and you can be sure that I made that speech happen. So look beyond powerful business leaders or celebrities … take a look closer to home and you may find that this is where your most inspiring role models are to be discovered – find out all you can and keep your own similar stories in mind next time you are tempted to give up.

Well, we've spoken about finding motivation, now let's see what can hold your motivation back. My number one would have to be: comparing yourself to others.

Regardless of who you are or what level you have achieved so far, it's human nature to compare yourself to others. We all think that others are doing a lot better than us. The people who you look up to and who impress you with their success in turn look up to their own competition and are always comparing themselves to it. Whatever our situation, whether a start-up, a blogger or makeup artist, someone working for a brand, or just in our day-to-day life, we always have to face competition. Including me.

When I started Rodial not only was I putting a lot of pressure on myself to get my brand off the ground, I also had to deal with the success of other brands coming out of nowhere and being 'overnight successes' much faster than me. And that could have made me want to quit right away. I was growing my business, step by step, while seeing all the other brands fast-forward their way to success. That was one of the most demotivating things I had to deal with.

These days starting a brand is so much easier. A new brand can set up an Instagram page, work it like crazy, get immediate recognition and sell direct-to-consumer (a fancy term for having their own website and not selling via third-party stores). I am not saying it's easy but I have seen brands being launched on Instagram and suddenly they amass millions of followers, tens of thousands of likes and instant buzz and recognition. I personally don't believe in anything instant, as I explain in *How to Be an Overnight Success* (spoiler alert: there's no such thing as an 'Overnight Success'). Anyone who comes in and becomes so successful has usually had a few failed careers before they finally made it. They have all faced failure large and small, but learned their lesson and moved on.

I know of a beauty specialist (no names!) who launched a makeup range. There was a lot of buzz around the launch and I have to admit that I and everyone else thought this was going to be the next big thing. It deserved to be. Then suddenly we stopped hearing about the range. Without any fanfare, it disappeared from the stores and no one talked about it any more. Scroll forward a few years and the beauty expert concerned moved on and set up another brand, and, in my opinion, armed with the invaluable experience of a set back (whatever the reasons), it worked out the second time.

That's why, when I look at competition that seemingly comes out of nowhere, I know there is probably a story of a failure or a setback or two and I think it's important to talk about them. The failures and the lessons we learn from them are the most valuable and important parts of learning to improve. The skinned knees we got on our first bike, the water we inhaled learning to swim, the twisted ankles trying to walk in McQueen's Alien shoes ... these are all vital life lessons (OK, maybe not the shoes), and the things we learn from doing it wrong are just as vital as those we learn from doing it right. Whatever does not kill us makes us stronger, right?

11

Even so, wherever I go I find people in all walks of life, but particularly business entrepreneurs, striving to portray themselves in the best possible light, and only very rarely will you hear the true, uncensored, warts-and-all story of how they came to be where they are today.

For example, I was listening to a beauty bloggers' panel. It was a great panel, but when it came to the question of 'how I made it as a beauty blogger' I got frustrated by some of the answers. I was well aware of some of the inside stories of what they went through to get where they are today ... and I was also well aware of the huge teams of people behind some of them: the agents, managers, publicists and so on who had helped them. One of the bloggers had a previous career in the industry before she started posting on YouTube and amassing millions of followers, but her advice to the audience could, in my view, have been more specific about all that. Instead, she just kept saying, 'Love what you do and work hard.' Which in itself isn't bad advice, but I would have liked there to have been more of a focus on the time, setbacks and teams of people who helped to get her to where she is today. I don't question talent. But everyone listening to this was thinking, *Well I love what I do and I work 24/7, so why am I not as successful as you?* I just think that all of us who have grown a successful career or business have a responsibility to give some practical advice ... and for me that means detail about the steps we have taken and the help that we have received along the way. We have a responsibility to help others become successful too. So next time you see a success story and you start doubting yourself, don't – and take it with a pinch of salt.

With people like me telling everyone how to make it happen, there is going to be lots of competition out there ... so how can you survive as a new brand? You don't have the big bucks the companies have, you don't have the

Instagram followers of a celebrity and you are not a start-up that struck gold with some massive investment. Is there a future for the rest of us?

Yes, there is! I had none of the above and here I am. I do recognise that the sense of injustice at those who 'had it easy' never quite goes away. I can't help but be aware of who the competition is and what they do – in fact, it's crucial for my business to keep up with what my contemporaries are up to – and yes, I still find myself coming up with excuses of why I can't be more successful than them. It is infuriating, but then I remind myself that I am following my own path, I have my own goals and my own way of achieving them.

I may have grown a lot more slowly but I have built a solid business over the years with some bestselling products, I have a good core team around me and still enjoy going to work every day. Being happy with what you do is more important than always comparing yourself to something different (I say 'different' not 'better') and feeling a lesser person. (So, perhaps that blogger's advice, 'Love what you do and work hard,' wasn't all bad!) And I use the competition to drive me but, if it gets to the point where following the competition becomes toxic, I make sure I take a step back and get them out of my life for a while. There are only so many times you can see someone's yacht party at Cannes before it starts to get you down. You can choose who you follow on social media and whose articles you read, and it's down to you to remove anything that doesn't create positive feelings and makes you feel like a failure. But also remember: admiring someone's success does not diminish your own.

I get lot of bloggers reaching out on Instagram at my @MrsRodial account saying that they feel they are always chasing something but never feel like they win. My advice is always to go back and look at yourself two years ago. Look at how you evolved. Compare yourself only to yourself

13

and your own personal progression. Remember, use your competition as your inspiration and nothing more. You can always draw energy from small successes. A positive comment on one of your IG posts, a nice email from someone you work with, a great meeting with a new person you've been dying to work with ... there will be many moments to draw on if you feel your positivity levels start to dip. Celebrate every little success to give you the energy to keep on going. And once things really start rolling, girl are you going to need the energy!

February 2018. I was in New York for my book launch. The week started with a book signing and a Q&A with the utterly iconic Alexa Chung at the Crosby Street Hotel, followed by store appearances, events and talk shows. The diary was booked by the hour and if that wasn't already crazy enough it was also New York Fashion Week. Of course, that was no surprise, we planned it that way. While it can sometimes be a gamble trying to make a splash at such a big event, and we had no illusions that we were anything but a very small fish in a very big pond, we knew that the right press and influencers would all be in town that week and it's important to get in front of the right people when you can ... no matter how few. It's the same principle that sends countless bands both known and unknown, signed and unsigned, to SXSW in Austin every year. You've got to go to where the deals are being made.

I wasn't new to New York Fashion Week – I love it there and as Rodial and my @MrsRodial profile had gained recognition, so had the invites I was getting to shows. Yes it was work, but it was always fun ... and great for me to see and be seen. As well as attending the shows, I usually like to go to a few parties and generally have a good time while I am there. I'd be crazy not to, right? Well, this time as well as my usual Rodial duties, such as meeting with the US team, meeting with makeup artists and beauty bloggers and launching new products, I had a book to promote. There was so much going on that I hardly had time to think, I needed to be 'on' and deliver at all times. I mean, I love talking to people but even I was starting to tire from the constant round of press activities, especially when I was basically saying the same thing over and over again. But this was really important, this was how I was going to get my book out there. I had a host of influential people coming to see me and I had to conserve my energy so I could give it my all when I needed to. At the end of a non-stop round of panels and filmed interviews, and with jet-lag looming, all I wanted to do was get back to my hotel room and catch up on my notes for the next day's sessions ... and catch up on *Kardashian* re-runs.

My hotel room was in sight and my PJs were calling me when my PR suggested we stop off and have a drink at the Stuart Weitzman party. There was no way I was up for this, but my PR, who is big on partying, talked/bullied/guilted me into going. I had very little defence against her arguments: 'It's going to be an early one ... you are already in hair and makeup ... we'll just stay for half an hour and show our faces ... Gigi Hadid was the face of their last campaign, there could be an interesting crowd.' Sigh ... you got me. Reluctantly I agreed and we diverted the cab. She is very persuasive. She'd be good in PR.

The event was being held in a new midtown Manhattan restaurant called the Pool – it's a gorgeous mid-century-modern space in the iconic old Four Seasons Pool Room. The fabulous high-ceiling room with the new collection of Weitzman shoes displayed prominently in the middle was already thronging when we arrived. I headed to the bar, bumping past models and swanky fashion editors as I went with the words of my PR 'just half an hour, just show our faces' front and centre in my mind. Waiting for my Perrier water (a waste of a free bar, I know, but I don't drink much), I could not help but notice that standing next to me was a supercool New Yorker with beautiful dark skin and bleached blonde hair. She looked amazing but, even so, this being me, the first thing I noticed was the Loewe Obi belt that I was so obsessed with last season and had sold out. 'I love your belt,' I said to her, 'too bad it sold out already.' 'Oh no,' she said, 'this is from the new collection ... it just dropped.' Accessory alert! Action stations! I was making a mental note to get online as soon as I left this party and order one. I was also thinking, *What a cool girl.*

Just then a photographer came by and said, 'Can I take a picture of you both?' And then more photographers arrived and suddenly there was a stampede of strobing flashguns, the usual street-style routine. *That was cute*, I thought, *two cool-looking girls in NY during fashion week.* As we parted I thought, *I don't know who this girl is, but she was really edgy and fresh and had a great vibe about her. She may be someone who could model for us, she may be someone who we could send some product to ... either way she's lovely and it can't hurt to stay in touch.* So I told her, 'Hey I love your style and I'd love to follow you on Instagram, what your handle?' '@saintrecords,' she says. It was only Beyoncé's sister, Solange Knowles.

So have Solange, Beyoncé and I become besties and hung out together? Well, no. (Like this is ever going to happen, but still, dream big ... make it happen!) So was it actually a waste of my time to attend that event? Was this one of the opportunities that come to nothing or one that will blossom?

Well, I believe it was one of the good ones. Connections were made, our photo together got my name out there

16

one more time, and who knows what other potential opportunities this could lead to? The ripples travel far out into the lake, after all. When unexpected things happen, you never know where they can take you, but if you don't grab them with both hands you'll never get anywhere. Was I motivated to go to the event? No, I think we've established that. But sometimes making that one small step, just doing it even if you are *not* motivated, is what it takes.

Am I always in the best mood? Do I have constant motivation? The answer and the reality is no. There are times (more than I care to admit) when I am presented with an opportunity such as this and totally don't feel like it ... oh how I would love to just finish my book, or catch up on my boxsets or alphabetise my handbag collection ... but no, I actually listen to my own advice and remind myself that I should never waste an opportunity. So I say yes and see what happens. To be perfectly honest not every opportunity is worth the effort, but how do you choose which is the lucky ticket? You can't. You have to be in it to win it, as they say.

So sometimes you have to say *yes* to opportunities that come your way, no matter what. Working full-time and having a family, I usually don't take the time to go out. I get invites for some cool events (as well as invites for the opening of an envelope which, I admit, I do politely decline) and it takes a lot of effort to get back home from work and go out again. It's not just the hair, makeup, a cute outfit. It's also the mental energy to go out there and be in my best mood, ready to mingle. That takes a *lot* of energy and at the end of a crazy day at the office I just don't feel like it and I don't imagine you would either. But experience has taught me that these opportunities can be golden. So I talk to myself very sternly in the bathroom mirror, have an espresso and get out there to make it happen.

I remember speaking to Poppy Delevingne when she hosted an event for Rodial a couple of years ago and asking her how she managed to make herself stand out from the competition. She told me that she would go out every single night, meet people and make those connections. Her answer is one of the things I always think of when faced with a 'Weitzman party' decision. So I am sorry to disappoint, but I am not a natural-born party animal. Most of the time I don't feel like going out and socialising but then something unexpected happens, I meet someone interesting and we may end up working together, or I hear something that gives me a new perspective, or I simply look good and get some nice pictures for my Instagram. Nine times out of ten something good happens when I put myself out there and make the effort.

So take hold of the opportunities that arise. However, do take note: the same rules regarding learning from your mistakes will come into play here. You'll probably go to more 'fail' events than 'win' events to start with, but you will soon learn, hone your radar and recognise when to say 'no' to things you know will not serve you and when to be open to the unexpected surprise!

Make it Happen Secret #1

10 Steps to Get You Fired Up

You are not born with motivation, you develop motivation. Motivation is like a muscle that you have to work out every single day. Well OK, if you have one day off, you can go back at it the following day but it's important to keep it going. Everyone is motivated by different things. Some by a title, status, a career or money, others by social recognition and Instagram followers. Nothing wrong with any of these, just be honest about what motivates you and always go back to it when your motivation starts running low. And since you asked, here are my top ten ideas to help you kickstart your motivation every single day, so you can make it happen.

1. Choose the area you want to motivate yourself: work, fitness, family or lifestyle. Put together a mood board. Go through magazines, books, online articles and cut out everything that speaks to you, as small or as crazy and unattainable as it may be now. Complete your board, sit quietly and imagine you have everything on that board. How does that make you feel? Look at your board when you start your day to get yourself motivated or as often as you need to make you refocus.
2. Write a list of three things that you are most proud of and how they made you feel at the time. It could be getting your dream job at your dream company,

or getting a deal that you were working on for a while or reaching a personal goal. Think about the details and how they made you feel, how you called your loved ones, how you celebrated. Bring those positive feelings to the fore and let them motivate you and give you the energy to work for your next goal.

3. Write a list of your three failures. Examine the circumstances of why they happened. What did you learn from them? What was the number one lesson you learned (and be honest!)? Now think about taking a new risk and ask yourself what will be the worst that can happen and whether you can apply one of those past lessons for a better result.

4. Keep a stack of positive messages. Every time I get a thank-you note or an email from someone saying they love my products or they were inspired by my speech or my book and how it impacted their life, I put it in a folder. When I have a bad day, I go back to the folder and remind myself of how I am appreciated and those positive feelings get me back on track.

5. Find a role model. Research people that do the job or things that you love, follow them on social media, find articles about them. Read biographies, listen to podcasts of successful people that you can relate to. These are people that you admire and feel good hearing about – so keep a close eye on them and when you have a challenging day go back to your research and think, *How would this person deal with my challenge?*

6. Attend conferences, trade shows and talks. You will get inspired and you will also find out about new trends in your industry, but not just that. A speaker may even be from a different industry and background, but something they say can resonate with you and can give you a new outlook and motivation for a fresh start. When you hear speakers talk about their own challenges (and believe me everyone has challenges in this world), you will realise that you are not alone. Also, being away from your office and home and in a different setup (out of your comfort zone – important!) with new people can give you the motivation to go back to work with a new sense of purpose.

7. Take action. Don't wait for the perfect moment or perfect execution before you take action. It's easier to take that first step, assess your performance, go back and do it better next time. Don't wait until everything is perfect as it may be too late.

8. Be consistent. Motivation is better if you keep your work consistent and do what you need to do daily. Some days you will do it with more effort and passion and other days it will be a schlep. It's harder to keep the motivation going when you stop taking action. Keep it going even when you don't feel like it. It will pay off.

9. When you are feeling down or not making as much progress as you wanted, go back a year or two years. See where you were at the time. If you compare yourself to how it all looked when you started, most likely you will appreciate the progress that you've made and will feel good about yourself;

you'll feel confident. Confidence is the best way to get your motivation back.

10. Remind yourself why you are doing what you are doing. Going back to the 'why' is important to help you get back on track.

2

Be a Goal Digger

London, September 2001. I am in a backroom at home. The room is tiny and just fits a small desk, a cupboard full of product and some lab samples. I am on the phone all day. If it's not the lab, talking about new products, it's a supplier discussing packaging. If it's not a customer wanting advice on the best skincare, it's a PR wanting a product image sent to them. My only real human interaction is with a bookkeeper who comes to see me once a week to do my accounts (and tuts and sighs disconcertingly while doing so). After working all the hours and weekends that exist I somehow bend time sufficiently to make my way to the stores to try to sell them my products. No rest for the wicked, but I can't think what I have done that quite deserved this. Welcome to Rodial. This is year one.

Fast forward. I am at a beautiful office space in the centre of London with open-plan seating and floor-to-ceiling windows. I have a proper office with a seating area for meetings and beautiful furniture. On the walls there are pictures of my campaigns with stars from Kylie Jenner to Sofia Richie. My team has grown to hundreds across the globe and I have created a second brand for the millennial customer called NIP+FAB that is taking the beauty market by storm. Welcome to the Rodial Group. This is year 18.

How do you go from a back office at home to a global beauty empire? Setting goals is what got me where I am today. A lot of people ask me that standard business forum question, 'What is your five-year plan?' I never had a five-year plan, but I always had a one-year plan ... and even that would be broken down by month, by week and by day. I would say, 'By the end of the year I would like to add three more stores.' That would be my target, and every single day I would take action to get me closer to this goal. Did I get three stores at the end of the year? I got two but this is still progress. The next year I would set a goal for five stores in the UK and one store internationally, and again, I would take action every day to get me there. Another goal would be to get two more staff at the end of the year if I reached X amount of sales. And if I reached half, I would still hire one more person. You get the picture: any progress is still progress. Every year, I would assess where I was and how to stretch the goal to something bigger and better. Did I get all my goals achieved? No. But it works both ways, Sometimes I would achieve very little, but then suddenly I would get an unexpected surprise and achieve much more than I set out to do ... although, to be fair that was more of a rarity. The point was that I kept going and kept on reminding myself of those goals, every single day.

Do *you* know exactly what your goals are? Let's say you have two people defining their goals in five years and one says, 'I want to be successful at what I do', and the other says, 'I want to be promoted to head of department, or make X amount of money.' Which one of the two do you think will get there? Which of the two knows what steps are needed to achieve their goals?

Think about what you want, where you want to be, what you want to achieve. Make it clear and simple. This will be the most important thing you do. You may already have your goal clearly in place – and that's why you are reading this book. If that is the case I say, 'Good! Well done you! Gold star!' If you haven't, that's OK, that's why I wrote this book: to give advice. So now, stop reading, put down the book and go and think about what you want to do.

You may say my goal is to be more successful, make more money, get fit. Is that enough? Not quite. You need to be accurate and precise about how you define success, making money or getting fit. You need to turn your dreams into bite-size measurable goals and take action to make them happen. Dreaming without goals is just wishful thinking.

Start writing your goals down *now*. Plan your goals for the year, split by month, week, day. This will be your motivational drive to make it happen. When you have daily goals, not only do you build a routine but you will feel in control of your destiny Every. Single. Day. Writing your goals down changes your attitude from being reactive to what's going on around you to being proactive and making it happen.

If you want to get fit by running on a treadmill, for example, write down how far you want to run and how fast, and your timeline. Write also how this would make you feel when you achieve your goal. Visualise yourself having achieved that goal. And break it down into small pieces. To achieve my goal, I need to go to the gym every Monday, Wednesday and Saturday. These days and times will go into my diary and I will work everything else around them. Make sure you always remember *why* you are doing this. When you feel like you are losing motivation, go back to what is driving you, find your purpose and stick to your goals. And sometimes, it's not just about the goal. It's about enjoying the process and being open to any exciting new surprises that come up along the way. Be in control of your dreams. Be in control of your goals. And Make It Happen.

Now there are times when you need to slightly adjust your goals. When you need to be realistic. You may have pursued one avenue and you are not getting results. It's important to periodically review your progress and adjust accordingly. It could be as simple as those days and times that you have scheduled to go to the gym aren't working out with the rest of your schedule, or you lose interest in running on a treadmill and need to run outdoors. It's OK. While you are pursuing your goals you still need to enjoy the process, so if something doesn't feel right, adjust. Or it could be that you were working on a specific work goal and you didn't get the desired outcome. There was a time when I started not liking gym classes, the instructors changed and I wasn't motivated any more, or my body stopped changing and needed to find a more challenging class. At those times you reset, do your research and set some new goals. The best goals are the ones that are being moved and adjusted to reflect your progress.

However, I do believe that setting a well-thought-out, achievable goal at the start of your journey is crucial. Only *you* know what *you* want to achieve, so I can't tell you what that might be but it's important that you give it some really thorough planning and consideration. I am calling them 'goals', but you may prefer 'key objectives' as this suggests more of an ongoing campaign of improvement. So, your planning should start with the 'ultimate goal' (run 5k, get a million followers, get a promotion, etc.) and then plotting the objectives along the way. It's a 'baby steps' approach but it works, as long as you are clear in your vision. As Lao Tzu's overused but nonetheless spot-on wisdom states, 'A journey of a thousand miles begins with one step.'

So, rule number one is be *specific* about your goals, and again, I reiterate, make sure you write them down so you can go back and remind yourself what they are when you need some extra motivation. Writing this book is a good example: if I waited for a time when I could have sat down and written 50,000 words in one go, it would never have happened. What I do is say to myself, 'I will put aside one hour every weekend and write down one page'. That's my goal. What ends up happening is that once I get myself into it, I end up writing more than one page. But the one-page goal works to keep me going and keep me motivated.

To make things easier, I'd recommend writing your goals down somewhere you can see them and be reinvigorated every day. Stick them on the fridge, have them as your screen saver, put them up in big neon letters on your wall, but do revisit them often – they are your motivator and your kick-starter every day, especially on the days that haven't gone so well.

Many people get super motivated and write their goals every year as a list of New Year's resolutions. It's a great idea, but it's not 'the be all and end all'. Everyone tends to feel that this is the time of the year for a fresh start, and why not? The year ahead is full of promise, we've probably had a nice break, maybe over-indulged a bit and this is the perfect time to make a change. The problem with those New Year's resolutions is that they very rarely go past March, mainly because they are vague in their purpose and the goal is poorly conceived (usually at precisely 11.59 pm on New Year's Eve). I don't mean to be a killjoy – please go on making New Year's resolutions if you want – but in order for you to achieve your goals, you need to know your yearly, monthly and daily goals. Can you do that? If the answer is still yes, then don't wait until New Year – do it now. Make it happen!

These goals need to be specific. If you say, I need to progress in my job, what does that mean? More responsibility, bigger scope of work, new skills, move to another department, get a promotion? You need to break it down and be absolutely clear what progress means. Likewise, if you say, I want to get fit, what does that mean? Give yourself a specific target and put together a plan of action of how to get there. Not a yearly plan; a weekly and a daily plan of how you will get there. When we plan our yearly sales targets at Rodial, we have a series of deadlines for hitting these goals. We break down the goals by month, by week, by day. We then communicate these to our sales teams and everyone takes responsibility for their own goals. They know what they need to sell per year, per month, per day, even per hour. If you break it down to the most basic level, everything looks so much more achievable. The same applies to your plans. Put down a deadline so you work on a plan to follow, one step at a time.

When you decide what you want to achieve, the questions you should ask yourself are simple:

- When? Break down your time into milestones – monthly, weekly, whatever helps, but do keep a strict timetable in mind. It is so easy to let things drift, especially when you are holding down a job or running a family while trying to work towards a new dream.
- Who with? Do you need to recruit a team? Do you need specialist help? I am not a science whizz, so I went and found a brilliant lab to help to create my products.
- What? What are the things that might get in your way? What are the conditions and limitations of your plan? Be honest with yourself.
- Why? Probably the biggest question of all. Make sure you know the answer to this – this is what will keep you focused on realising your goal more than anything.

Be specific about what you want to achieve, set your path, set your markers and deadlines, and be prepared to review, reassess and adapt ... but keep true to your goal.

When working on a goal, I am all about taking small steps consistently. I look at when I work out. I go to conditioning classes where you can choose the weights you want to work with. I know that if I go heavy, I will exhaust myself to the point of not returning to the class for another week. What I do is work with lighter weights but I can go back to the class the next day and the day after. Small daily improvements work better for me and my fitness goal rather than going hard on one day and doing it ad hoc.

This reminds me of the Kaizen principle. This is the way of working that was behind Japan's huge success in business and manufacturing in the mid-twentieth century. In Kaizen, the workers in Japan's offices and factories were challenged to think, 'What extremely small step could I take to improve the process or product?' The world domination of products with 'made in Japan' stamped on the bottom soon followed.

There is a strong reason why this works, and it comes neatly back to those deep-seated instincts to run away from sabre-toothed tigers. Taking small, almost imperceptible steps allows you to gently sneak past your inbuilt caveman guardian of your fears. So, if you think your goal is unachievable, stop, break it down into the smallest steps and you can get to your final destination.

I have spoken earlier about the importance of setting your timetable. After all, time is money! Deadlines give you focus and can galvanise you into action just when it seems your energy is slipping. But don't be too hard on yourself if you miss a few. Throughout my journey of writing this book, I may have missed a weekend or two, or even a whole month, when my mind was somewhere else and it was hard for me to focus. It's OK, I didn't beat myself up for not writing but, when I felt my mind was back on it, I did sit with my laptop and start writing a few words and got myself back on track. If you are too rigid about hitting the targets when you fail it can actually be very demoralising. You need this to be an enjoyable, positive experience, not a mad race against the clock. This is particularly relevant if you have a team. Don't be too inflexible: you need to keep morale high. If you don't meet the deadline, simply review, reassess, reset

31

the clock. The key is to keep moving forward. Sometimes at Rodial, we may miss the target for a week or a month. We reset and come up with a new plan of action. We may end up getting a better sales month and make up for any deficit we had. As much as you plan there are always setbacks. Take them as an opportunity to reset, which can give you renewed energy and motivation.

How do you ensure you stick to your goals? One of the reasons people tend to give up on their goals (in typical New Year's resolution fashion) is that they have forgotten why they committed to them in the first place. At times when I have a hard week at work, I do get demotivated and negative thoughts come into my mind that make me almost give up on my goal and quit. (Well, I can't really 'quit' to anyone as I own the company, but I guess the equivalent would be those feelings I still have, when it gets tough, of wanting to just disappear!) It's at these times I try to remind myself why I am doing what I am doing. What I love about my job. I think back to some of my best moments and the successes I have had. I often go back and read a great piece of press that put a smile on my face or recall some bit of positive feedback from a customer using our products. I have to go back and remind myself why I am doing what I am doing and get myself back on track.

This is what you need to do. Know your goals, put a plan in place and always remind yourself of the reason. Now, I may be painting a bleak picture here and making all of this seem like it's a huge challenge. I don't mean to paint that picture: I am just underlining that these are the strategies you need to make it happen. There are those for whom risk and uncertainty are huge motivators. These lucky souls thrive on challenges and beating odds, and if you are one of these people then that is great, but you still need to have a structure and be specific.

So your goals should be realistic and achievable but don't cheat on the dream. Also, have 'stretch goals', a few 'if onlys' to make the path more exciting. There is a fine balance between having realistic goals and goals that come out of dreaming big. You need to look at both. When I started writing my first book, *How to Be an Overnight Success*, my goal was to publish the book by a certain date. I made that happen by writing a little, even if it was a page, every weekend I could, and by hustling and sending emails to different publishers, and then doing all the follow up. My stretch goal was to make it a bestseller. Which I did, two months after publishing it. Having a realistic goal made me focus on the day-to-day, while the stretch goal was a bigger dream to achieve, which took a bit longer, and I allowed myself more time rather than expect them both to happen at the same time, which was unrealistic and would have been disheartening.

Make it Happen Secret #2

10 Steps to Become The Ultimate Goal Digger

1. Write down your personal and professional goals on a piece of paper; start with the big picture.
2. Break down these goals in smaller bites, how these would look monthly, weekly and daily.
3. Keep a summary of your goals on a small piece of paper and carry it with you to remind yourself of them as often as needed.
4. Look at your daily goals and decide whether they are achievable. Especially at the beginning, you need to make progress so you can stick with them.
5. Start small and grow the goals as you go so that you gain confidence by achieving the easier goals and sticking with them.
6. Review your goals and adjust them as needed. Your goals are dynamic, and as your life and circumstances change you need to be able to adjust your goals to make them relevant.
7. Reward yourself periodically for achieving some of the smaller goals; celebrate small successes as they come.
8. Create a vision board with your stretch goals, which you will review every few months to remind yourself to dream big. This will motivate you even more to achieve your daily goals.
9. Keep consistency. If you miss your goal for a few days, start afresh. When our team has a bad week

34

in sales, we always turn over a new leaf. A new day, a new week, a new month is coming.

10. Always have a deadline for your goals and measure yourself against it. A sense of urgency can be a big motivator.

3 Nothing Fabulous Happens Inside a Comfort Zone

So you may be stuck in your career, you may love what you do but you want to progress, you may want to change careers or change direction in your life. You may look at this and think this is a massive task to undertake and you keep on delaying it until you are 100 per cent motivated. You may feel a change is big and daunting and start procrastinating. Just get started ... that is all you need to do. Take the first step, even if it's a small one. If you want progress, do not delay. Don't wait around for the day you think you are ready for the giant leap. Take small consistent steps now and every day. I guarantee that you will be surprised at the progress. Break your goal into small pieces and start attacking one step daily and consistently.

To be successful, you just have to get started. Make that first move. Action brings action, and action brings success.

It was my eighth year of running the business, things were ticking along nicely, but I felt that we had plateaued and were just, well, ticking along! I wanted to do something that would take us to the next level and get our name out there ... but what? We had a bit of money but not the sort that could suddenly buy TV and mass media campaigns. We needed to be cleverer than that. What amazing press event could we create to celebrate our anniversary and crucially get us in front of not only more people, but the right people?

Every day I'd pick up the paper or see pictures online of beautiful people on red carpets. It seemed that all the mega brands were hosting lavish parties and I wanted Rodial to play on that field. I had a meeting with my team and we came up with the idea of hosting *the Rodial Beautiful Awards*. It was a crazy idea ... but we didn't know back then how crazy! The Rodial office only had a team of about ten people at the time, all with very full timetables all crucial to keeping the business on track. We knew that we

39

were nowhere near the size of company to take on such a massive project, but the members of my team were up for it and, as always, we said, let's make it happen! The objective in the first year was to establish the awards, invite a few celebrities and create some buzz for the brand. Simple, right?

Well, it was a steep learning curve, that's for sure. When I think of our first awards, I am very embarrassed at what we produced. We knew we needed a venue that would fit with our brand – cool, stylish and of the moment – so we got a space at the Sanderson hotel in central London. The Sanderson is a striking modernist building, with interiors designed by Philippe Starck and packed with surrealist art and furniture … it's achingly trendy. It was perfect. We booked a beautiful space, sent out the invites and waited for the RSVPs to roll in, and we were pleased to find that we were getting some great responses. This was the biggest thing we had done this far … and it was stretching us. As well as the time there was the money and we had spent all of it just booking the space. Now, the space on the night looked beautiful, but with no budget to dress or brand, it was just a space. This was a huge error on my part. I had thought about it, but when I looked at the costs, I decided it would be fine without … but now, standing in the room just before we started, I realised what a mistake I had made. This was our chance to get our name in front of people in a big way, and our name was nowhere! An awards event with no branding … it was embarrassing.

Through our connections we had managed to get some strong names there, from Paloma Faith to Jade Jagger, and with great energy and a lot of hustle over the preceding weeks, we had filled the room with cool people … a room where the word 'Rodial' was noticeably absent. I never actually heard anyone saying, 'What's this awards for again?'

40

out loud but I was convinced it was happening and found myself desperately trying to make sure I slipped 'Rodial' as many times as possible into every conversation I had that night. It was exhausting! All that aside, we did come out with a win. We managed to generate some decent publicity for the brand through all of the calls we made, even to those who didn't come. We had established a starting point and sent the message that Rodial is now hosting big awards.

So, for our second year we not only had a bit more budget but we were also starting to get calls from agents who wanted to secure invites for their clients. The idea was working. Now we had to build on it. First of all ... branding! I made sure that this time we got a Rodial-branded 'step and repeat' – it's like a wall covered in multiple logos – perfect for the publicity shots of guests and celebs and now a staple feature of all parties, events, awards and 'post-match' sports interviews. Every single person would have their photo taken surrounded by the Rodial logo. I also increased the drinks budget: it was a party after all. The awards themselves were not really any bigger, but these small but important changes helped us stay in the eye of the beauty press, celebrities, agents and influencers. The photos did the rounds and we could see that this was working. The event gave people a reason to talk about Rodial without us having to do a hard sell. Our name was starting to make the right connections.

In our third year we started work much earlier, pretty much as soon as year two was done. Now we were serious, the formula worked but we couldn't stay still and if we were going to grow the awards we couldn't do it in the way we had done before. Myself and all the office staff had just been squeezing in the planning alongside our other work, i.e. running the company. This was neither professional nor fair to my team. So we decided to hire a party planner to advise us on how to do this better and a production company to

41

create a show. Instead of us guessing what we might need, we were having production meetings with experts who did this every day. There were plans of the stage, there were scripts, branding, rehearsal schedules. Now we were going somewhere! When the news came in that we would have Elle Macpherson and Whitney Port attending, the phones and messages just blew up and now it seemed that every agent was calling us to get invites for their VIP clients.

By year four we were in full control. The budget went even further, we hired a celebrity booker and had some of the biggest names, including Kate Moss, win awards. That was the year we got tons of press, people were fighting to get on our list and the *Rodial Beautiful Awards* became one of the key events in the social calendar. It had taken us four years to be where we needed to be. We started small (and, as you have seen, a bit pathetic) but we knew that this was something worth getting right. This was a key objective on the road to achieving our goal. So, even though we were at times overwhelmed by the challenges, we just did it anyway. We kept growing and kept learning and kept improving our format.

So, what I learned was that sometimes you need to make the first move even if you haven't figured it out 100 per cent. As we know, we all have a fear of failure, the voice that tells us that we are not ready for it, that it won't be perfect and that we should wait until the time is right. But the more you try and the more you fail, the better you get at knowing when to take the risk.

As with everything in my life, I always learned along the way. I started Rodial and had no clue of how you start a business and had no background in product development. I made more mistakes than you could ever imagine, from ugly packaging to working with the wrong suppliers to hiring the wrong people. I've made mistakes that cost me

42

time, money and threatened my reputation. People ask me all the time, 'If you were to start again, how would you do things differently?' Surprisingly, I would do the exact same thing. Learning from your mistakes is the best training you can ever have, it made me who I am today. It's trial and error. I have this discussion with my husband all the time when we talk about our two boys. He would sit them down and talk to them for hours on how they should do this and how they should do that with a detail that goes to the nth degree, and I say to him, just tell them the basics and then let them make their own mistakes, this is the only way they will learn. When I began, I read endless books on how to start and run a business, books that showed me what to do every step of the way ... but I still made every mistake in the world, and I expect you will too. My message here is not to be downhearted but to learn from these mistakes.

So how do you fight through failure and disappointment? It can be really difficult to pick yourself up and get back on track sometimes. I know! We all say to ourselves, 'I don't know enough about this, I am not ready about that and so I will delay taking action.' We procrastinate. We delay dealing with a task to give ourselves an excuse if we end up making a total mess of it. With procrastination, we sabotage ourselves and our success. We erect our own barriers to success to protect ourselves from hurting our ego, in case we fail. How can you beat this? One strategy is 'divide and conquer'. Usually the tasks that we delay doing are the least exciting ones ... you know, doing the Christmas shopping, laundry, exercise, paying the bills, taking out recycling. (Wow, I am depressing myself just writing those things down!) However, if you break the task down into small manageable bites and tackle them one by one you will find them easier to get through. This goes back to my previous point on using small steps to 'sneak past' your fearful, deep-rooted fight-or-flight responses. Make a list of those manageable bites and start ticking them off as you go down the list. Ticking things off a list is very satisfying, to the point that sometimes I start my 'to do' lists with 'make a to-do list' just so I can have the satisfaction of ticking that one off straight away.

It happens all the time, even now at work. There may be a tough project that I need to work on and it's not going to be creative or fun but I know I need to get going with it. The way I deal with it is to take one small action. My usual action is sending that first email. It could be as simple as emailing my team to say, 'Let's set a meeting to talk about this project, are you available at 3pm today?' The minute that email goes out, I have taken the first step and we are heading in the right direction. We would sit down and start talking through the project and I may hear some interesting thoughts, and we'll start taking the next steps to get it off the ground. Yes, it is as simple as sending out that first email. It's your first step. Legit.

So just get started. You won't have it perfect at the beginning. But if you wait to get it perfect you will miss the boat.

Nothing drives me more than taking on a new project that I know nothing about and I just need to figure it out. Like when I decided I wanted to launch a podcast. Why? I got such great feedback from *How to Be an Overnight Success* and have started so many conversations with readers like you. I love meeting people who have read my book. We would meet at book signings or I would get comments on my @MrsRodial Instagram account and there were always tons of questions and suggestions. But at events there is never enough time, and on instagram everything is communicated in short form ... we weren't quite chatting in emojis but near enough! I found it frustrating that I couldn't talk longer and in more depth.

44

I wanted to be able to continue conversations on another platform, where we could chat and analyse things in a bit more depth: to really look deeper into what inspires us, what bothers us and what entertains us. I wanted to find a platform to be with my readers and followers more often and give them more dynamic content.

I decided against YouTube for the simple reason that I want to focus on what I do best, which is talking and analysing and being real. I didn't want the focus of the discussion and comments to be about what we look like or how well we have accessorised. I wanted to record without worrying about being in full-on hair and makeup and just focus on what I was going to say. I'm a big fan of podcasts myself: they are my number one choice of listening on my way to work or the gym. So a podcast was the way to go.

Now where should I start? I knew nothing about podcasts, apart from being an avid listener. What would it be about? What should the title be? How often do I publish (or 'drop an episode' if we want to speak the lingo)? Should I have guests? What equipment do I need? Where do you even publish podcasts? Would anyone even listen to them? These and a thousand other questions populated my list of how to achieve this.

I did what I always do. Start researching. You would be surprised at how much info you get from typing 'How to start a podcast' on Google. I furiously read the first 20 articles and then went on Amazon and bought a book on 'How to Podcast'. I didn't find the book particularly helpful but I did get a couple of tips.

I knew the podcast was going to be about 'Overnight Success' (which we know doesn't exist but it was in keeping with the irony of my book title), but where do I start? Who can help me put this together?

My sister was in town for a few days and she is always discovering and recommending new things for me. Like all sisters she thinks that she is the cool one … I'm just copying her. I've learned to come to terms with it. So on this particular visit she arrived and presented me with a bunch of new magazines that I had never heard of. 'Here you go,' she said, 'got you some inspiration.' I was busy that day, stressed over a work thing, so said a quick thank you and put the magazines aside.

A few days later, my sister was gone and I still hadn't even looked at this pile of mags. It was on the following Sunday morning, after reading the Sunday papers (which is my Sunday highlight … I am obsessed with weekend papers and supplements), I reached out for those magazines. The one that stood out was the *Courier* magazine, describing itself as 'reporting on modern business and start-up culture'. (It's a great magazine, by the way. If you are a budding entrepreneur and you want to find about what's new and cool in business and stories of other start-ups, this is the place to go.) I opened it and I was hooked. You know there are those magazines you start flicking through looking for an interesting article to read and before you know it you are looking at the last page of the magazine and there was nothing worth your time? Well, the *Courier* wasn't like that. I was reading literally Every. Single. Page. Halfway through the magazine, I bump into an article about podcasts and a studio in east London that does all the production. I don't remember if it was raining on that Sunday morning (it usually is in London) but it was like the sun had just come out. Here in one article were pretty much all the things I needed. I moved into ultra-high gear. Within moments I had found that studio on Instagram, slipped them a DM and next day we were talking with the producer. We set up a meeting at their east London studio (always an interesting cultural excursion from west London, instantly making me feel cooler and ten years younger. (That's your FOC [free of charge] anti-ageing tip. You're welcome.)

In my head the whole thing was a done deal, but in reality I didn't know how we would get on. What if we hated each other? Well, no going back now. The worst that could happen would be an expensive Uber ride (east London is far), a good coffee (east London coffee *is* better than in the west) and a bad meeting. The coffee *was* great, the Uber ride *was* expensive, but that meeting went great! We didn't hate each other; within 15 minutes we started talking about potential episodes, and within an hour I said, 'Why don't we record the pilot next week?'

A week later, I had my pilot for my *Overnight Success* podcast (all the episodes are available on Apple Podcast, Spotify and all the popular podcast platforms). And the rest is history.

Was I 100 per cent ready to start my podcast? No. Did I have all the tools I needed? I didn't. But I knew enough to get started. I will probably listen to that first pilot and cringe a year later but who cares? I had made a start. Every recording makes me better and there is a learning curve. But there needs to be a start. There needs to be a moment when you think, *I don't know it all but I know enough to take the plunge, whether it be at work, in a career, or relationship.* There is a moment in every plan when delaying it ends up costing you more in the long run than just making a start, taking the risk and learning from it could ever do. I could have waited another year but I may have missed the boat or lost the interest and excitement I had for this new project. Strike while the iron is hot.

When I started the business, one of the first things I needed to do was secure investment. I was looking at other beauty brands around me and the way they would do it is write a business plan, present to potential investors, secure an investment to fund the business and live happily ever after (sometimes). I always seem to be reading this same story in the news: this company got X millions of funding; the beauty market is really hot and investors are looking to pour millions into the beauty industry; X founder of a beauty brand became a billionaire, etc. Doing what you love and making lots of money is a dream come true, right? So with my pre-Rodial start in the business and investment world, writing a business plan, putting together financial forecasts and presenting to investors would be a walk in the park, surely? If anyone could do this, it would be me. Full of confidence I hired a freelance graphic designer to put together a logo and mock up packaging for the range, and armed with a glossy PowerPoint presentation I was ready to go!

I contacted twenty investors, received six responses, organised three meetings and got zero investment. Zero. I got rejected by every single investor. As always, I like to ask for feedback: 'You don't have a background in beauty'; 'The market is too competitive'; 'We can't see your point of difference'; 'It's not the right time for us.' I was shattered. I felt a failure. I started losing faith in myself and my idea. It wasn't even about not getting the investment. In my mind, if those people didn't see the value in my business then my idea was worthless.

What did I do? I thought to myself, *I could wait another six months, rewrite the business plan and approach these and new investors again.* But what would have changed? I decided to take the plunge and start my business without external investment, with £20,000 savings and bootstrapping the business, day by day, month by month. Cash was tight but in hindsight this really helped me invest in the right things and grow my business organically.

I just got started and never looked back.

Make it Happen Secret #3

10 Steps to Get You Started

Sometimes we delay starting a project that looks massive and complicated. Get it started any way you can, make small progresses and you'll be surprised with the results. These are my top ten tips to get you started on any new project:

1. Break the project down into small bites. Put a list of those small bites together and promise yourself to tackle one a day minimum. It's the process of marginal gains. Assess your progress at the end of the week. When I started Rodial, there was so much to take care of, especially as I was a one-woman show doing it all myself. I would break down all the different areas I needed to address from lab work, to sales, to PR, to accounting, and focused on just one per day. At the end of the week I would review my progress and start fresh the following week.

2. The first step is the hardest. What I do to get a project moving is make the decision to send that first email to a key person. I recently decided on a repackaging project that would be very complicated and would involve a lot of different teams, so I sent that first email to my design team with the subject 'Repackaging Project' and a message, 'Let's all connect to discuss.' I was delaying making a start but by sending this email I got my team already thinking about it and that was the first step. And then

49

everything flowed. Discussion is good if you have other people involved. It gives them ownership and encourages their input.

3. Do your research. Find out how other people did what you are planning to do. Read online articles, books, listen to podcasts and watch YouTube videos. When you hear other people talking about how they got on, you will get inspiration and strength to do it too. They are normal people who Made It Happen and that's very inspiring.

4. Limit distractions. Distractions can be in the form of people around you or your phone beeping with constant notifications. I do my best work when I find a quiet space without distractions and I switch off my phone.

5. Group your meetings around a certain time and leave time for your actual work. I never pack a day full of meetings; if I can do it my way I will leave the morning free for creative thinking and big projects, and leave the afternoon for meetings. So I always find quality time for big projects.

6. Announce the project on social media. If it's not confidential, of course, announcing a big decision on social media is a way to commit yourself to it. I love posting motivational quotes on my @MrsRodial account, which usually relate to what I am going through that day, and motivate myself while also connecting with my audience.

7. Don't wait until everything is perfect, because it won't be. There will never be the ideal time to make a new start, whether that is starting a new job, a new business or a family. Make the decision and

then make everything else work around it. I didn't get an investor to back my business and started on a tight budget. It wasn't ideal, especially since a lot of my competition had bigger budgets, but I made it work to my advantage and became more creative as this was all I had.

8. Never compare yourself to others but always compare yourself to where you started. There will always be people that are smarter, prettier, more successful. Be inspired by others but only compare yourself to yourself and where you started. This is the only progress that matters. I couldn't help comparing myself to other brands and founders, and it wasn't helping. I still do at times, I can't help it, but then I always try to look at myself a few years ago and appreciate my own progress.

9. Self-doubt is healthy: we all self-doubt ourselves at times. No one is perfect. Analyse where your self-doubt is coming from, identify any weaknesses that you may want to work on and improve yourself, but don't dwell on it much. Let it go.

10. Take a meditation break. At the beginning everything seems like a mountain and we all feel like we are sinking at times. Take a few minutes to meditate when you feel overwhelmed. There are a lot of great apps out there that will ground you and make that first step seem achievable.

4

They Want You to Quit. Don't

Failure and rejection are two subjects that are very close to my heart. I have faced rejection time after time in my career. And I want to talk openly about this as I feel that very few people admit they've been rejected. If you have read my first book, *How to Be an Overnight Success*, you will know that I am very open about all the rejection that I faced while building my business. How I got fired from my job, how I didn't get funding and how I got rejected by every single retailer. And you know what? Every time I talk openly about rejection, I feel very liberated. I feel empowered. Rather than being embarrassed, I feel that by sharing my rejection with you all I bring a positive message that rejection and success can co-exist.

I listened to Lady Gaga give an Oscar acceptance speech recently and it deeply resonated with me. She talked about working hard for a long time and that success is not about winning an Oscar, it's about not giving up, it's about fighting for your dream. You get rejected a lot of times but what matters is how many times you stand up and being brave enough to keep on going.

You might think that you are the only person in the world that gets rejected. You are wrong. Regardless of who we are, where we are in our career or where we have been, we all face rejection. Every. Single. Day.

A couple of months ago, I got an email from the producers of a very popular business-related TV show here in the UK. You know the type: plucky small business contestant enters a room to dramatic music and meekly pitches their world-changing business idea to a panel of sphinx-like 'seen-it-done-it' entrepreneurs and moguls ... will they rip the poor hopeful to shreds or will they rip each other to shreds for a chance to invest? It's basically like the Roman Colosseum in pinstripe suits. Needless to say, I love it! I've been a huge fan of these shows for years, so imagine

55

my excitement when the email arrived to ask if I would be interested in auditioning to be a new panel member on the show. I could see the camera shots as I made my debut ... a swish of Balenciaga, a click of heels, a close-up of my inquisitive, immaculately groomed eyebrow, pan out to reveal dramatic backlit silhouette. Cue titles. Oh yes, this was definitely for me. I'd already had a small taste of this world when I appeared as a guest mentor on *Project Runway* in the US and I was definitely up for more. I mean, what could be more perfect, I love business and I love showbiz. This could be life changing, this would make me a household name (not easy when it's Hatzistefanis). When I started in business I had never even considered heading down this path and certainly hadn't been chasing this, but here we were, an email out of the blue meant that someone had thought, *She'd be good for this* – I was so flattered and thrilled that I put the brakes on everything else for the day and called the producers.

On the call I learned that maybe the email wasn't that special. It seems I was one of several hundred potential business leaders they had contacted. Ah yes, but are they as perfect for this as me? Have they got my 'make it happen' attitude? I went in my positive, assertive mode and prepared with my answers. I closed the call by saying: 'Give me a chance to do the screen test!' And they did!

My self-belief and positive approach had worked. I was making this happen. In a very short time I was selected out of those hundreds of other people to a final 'call-back' screen test (a call back is like an audition for those who have made the shortlist) with just a handful of other hopefuls. This was now my new goal, and I started working for it as I did with all my goals ... I was on it 24/7. My life stopped and it suddenly was all about preparing for that show. Every minute of the day that I wasn't working or sleeping, I was

56

watching old episodes, reading interviews, dissecting every word and getting my strategy right. What kind of a judge would I be? What would my character be? What will be my killer questions? How should I challenge the other judges? Am I in or out?

The day of the screen test arrived and I was a warrior. I was so ready. I looked the part, I felt the part . . . I was beyond ready for my screen test. And I killed it! I was confident, delivered great soundbites and made the producers laugh. That's got to be a good sign, right? Everyone said how amazing I did. I walked out of the studio on a high and began clearing my schedule for the next two months of filming.

A week later, I got rejected.

How did I feel? Well, not great. I was *so* close to making it. Seriously, I genuinely thought that I could bring it if I got selected, so was genuinely shocked by the rejection. In the days that followed I went through the five traditional stages of grief.

First, shock and denial (they must have phoned the wrong person . . . they can't have meant to reject me, can they?). Then anger (you *idiots* . . . I'd have been *amazing*!). Then came stage three, the bargaining (the usual churn going round and round in my head searching for an explanation). I paced the office reasoning with myself that compared to the other judges on the show I surely had a more contemporary and current angle, and I definitely speak to a younger demographic of women entrepreneurs. Through my social media accounts I could have made the episodes more interactive with me hosting live Twitter chats as the episodes go on air. I thought I knew exactly what the show needed to make it current and exciting, but I guess I didn't. Then came the next stage, depression (I must look weird on camera, that's the only explanation). So what about the final stage, acceptance? Well, I'm not quite there yet and here is why.

Rejection sucks. You have put a lot of work, your heart and soul into this and you are so close to the finish line. And then boom, you get rejected!

A lot of people try to make you feel better. They say: 'This happened for a reason.' Or 'There are bigger and better things coming your way.' That's just BS.

I don't think that not being selected to be on a national TV show happened for a reason. And I certainly don't think that a bigger TV show is just around the corner waiting for me. But what I do think is that every rejection is a time to reset. Time to take stock of what you're good at. What you can improve on. Reset your goals. Redefine your strategy. As with everything in life, I never put myself in a victim position. I don't accept rejection: I use rejection to fire me up to chase my dreams even harder.

Many people tend to blame others when they get rejected. I could have fallen back on excuses: it's the producers' fault, or they made a mistake and I was the best choice ... I could find a million reasons and a million ways to blame others, but the reality is this may have nothing to do with me. I don't know why I got rejected and it's still too raw for me to try to process it, but it could be anything. It could be that I still have a full-time job and they were looking for someone with more free time, or perhaps they were looking for someone older or more conservative, I don't know and it doesn't really matter. I am here now and I use the shock of this rejection to take me to my next goal, my next project, my next risk.

They also say that something good always comes out of something bad. The old silver linings playbook. If you know anything about me you know that I am not sitting still waiting for something good to miraculously come up because I deserve it. I had this amazing experience of being on the final line-up, being considered for an iconic national TV show. That was a massive deal for me. And in a way, being part of that final was enough validation for me and even if I didn't make it at the end, let me just take a minute and be grateful about the opportunity to audition and everything that I learned along the process. OK, maybe this is acceptance!

Every experience I have had, good or bad, led me to the next. And every *no* I got made me try harder to get to a *yes* next time. I embrace rejection and challenges as a way to evolve, to get better, to be ahead of the game. If you asked me, 'Would you go through this TV show experience again, even if you knew you had no chance of getting it?' Absolutely! I put myself out there, worked hard to deliver the best possible outcome and genuinely enjoyed the experience! And now, here I am, sharing my rejection story with you and, I hope, giving you a positive message. Was I deflated? Yes! Will I give up on chasing my next goal? Absolutely not.

What I learned over time is that success is wrapped in rejection. It's all about taking risks, putting yourself out there and developing very thick skin. You *will* fail at times but you *will* pull yourself together and get back at it.

In all honesty, this was nothing new. I get rejected every single day. Where do I start? Investors, retailers, employees, associates. My career has been a series of rejections with some breakthroughs and successes in between. I could have quit at any time. Believe me, it's not easy. You're working hard, you're putting 100 per cent of yourself out there but the results are just not happening. Business is just like that. You take one step forward and two steps back. It's a game of snakes and ladders. You clamber up to one success and think you've made it and then, on the next roll of the dice, a snake awaits and down you go. (Well, in my case a snake was a good thing but you get the point.)

Rejection is just part of life. Regardless of your background, experience, goals in life, rejection happens to us every single day. When I started the business, I always had a dream of getting my products in a luxury department store. I was naive and thought it would be easy. Just put a few products in a beautiful gift box, send them to the buyers, follow up with a call and email, set a meeting and you're in business. That is exactly what I did, full of confidence that they would immediately see that this was the next big thing. No mere human could resist my beautiful product and my sky-high levels of self-confidence and belief, could they?

Well, apparently they could. My calls went unanswered and I got no emails back. I have to admit I was devastated. A year went by and I did the exact same thing. However, this time I got an answer, 'Thanks for getting in touch … but I am afraid we don't have space for your product at this time.' OK, it wasn't quite the response I wanted, but at least they acknowledged my existence. That's progress, right? Every year I did the same thing: I'd decide that this was the year my products would be in that luxury store. This was the time. And every year I'd get the same knock back. I'd call, they'd say there was no space, I would be disappointed and then get back to my other sales. The next year, after seven years of trying, I went through the whole process again: I got in touch, they responded and I was preparing myself for disappointment again … but wait, hold on, let me read that email again. Oh wow … they want a meeting! I went to the meeting, they saw that my products had a point of difference and how passionate I was about them, and in what seemed like no time we were launching in the store.

To this day I do not know what changed or what I did differently. It could be that actually there really was 'No space' up until then. It could be that I ground them down, or got them on a good day. I don't know and I didn't dare ask at the time. (Now I would!)

It was a humbling experience to have to knock on that door seven years in a row with a lot of rejection, but the key is not to take it personally. And in a way, getting a *no* drove me to work harder, improve my products, get myself and my business in a better position so the next time I knocked on that door I could show them my progress.

You can't avoid rejection. Life has its ups and downs and rejection is part of life. There are people who are open about rejection and others who are not. When you look at someone and think they have the perfect life, career, etc., always know that they too are facing their own rejections. Whenever you have goals and try to achieve something, rejection comes hand in hand with hustle. The only way to avoid rejection is to change nothing and just stand still, which is also a goal of sorts. What option are *you* going to choose? Working hard to achieve your goals and facing a lot of rejection along the way or standing still, having no goals and dreams and a safe, boring life that will bring you less rejection?

Hands down, I always go for chasing my dreams and putting myself up for rejection. I chase higher goals that keep me on my toes and make me grow and accept that that I will have to face rejection along the way.

When you are young and just starting out, rejection can seem like the end of the world. I kept on thinking, *I worked so hard, I am hustling every single day, why can't people see this and give me a chance?* And I would get mad. Mad at the people who rejected me and mad at myself for being in this position and feeling like a victim. *Poor me, why is this happening to me, it's not my fault.* This wasn't a healthy way of dealing with rejection. The best way of dealing with rejection is to learn from it. The way I look at it now is that I just wasn't the right person at that time. The fit just wasn't right. Maybe I have changed, maybe I have learned, maybe it's a bit of both, but I look at rejection differently now and although I joked around with the five stages of grief earlier I do believe this process can help you. However, I have developed my own more concise version, it's a set of tools to deal with these situations that really works.

When I am faced with rejection, instead of five, I usually go through three phases:

Phase 1: Shock. I have built myself up for achieving that goal and the minute I hear the news of rejection, I am in a state of shock, I almost cannot believe it. I get this tightness in my stomach and a real feeling of loss. It might seem strange to feel loss for something you never had, but in my mind I was counting on this, I had made space for it and not getting it takes me a step back. A thousand thoughts go through my mind. This is not the time to take action as anything I do would be on impulse and I wouldn't want to do anything rushed that I'd regret later. However, it is worth logging initial thoughts to assess with a cooler head as sometimes those gut reactions can help inform your later plan. Anger and rejection make you act in weird ways. Depending on the type of rejection, the shock stage lasts from 24 to 48 hours.

Phase 2: Acceptance. The second stage is the acceptance of what has just happened. I have digested the news and accepted it. Still not happy but I look at it from a more objective perspective, with the initial reaction and emotion gone. The important things come into focus; the unimportant melts away. Now I can really see more clearly. This lasts another 24 to 48 hours.

Phase 3: Action. This is the more interesting phase for me. Once I have gone through the shock and accepted the situation, I challenge myself to find ways to overcome this hurdle. It could be coming up with a plan B to achieve the same result in a different way, it could be improving my skills/products/team to be in a better position next time I tackle it or it could be approaching the subject from a different angle and perspective. This is my favourite phase: I am reinvigorated by this new challenge, I will not be beaten! During this phase, I sometimes surprise myself, often coming up with ideas and creative solutions that I never would have considered in the calm, confident atmosphere before the rejection hit me.

I have gone through these stages so many times in my life that these days I know what's coming. I know that I am angry and disappointed at myself when things don't go my way but I also know that I will get over it. And I also know that I will end up coming up with a bunch of new ideas and directions that will take me to a different path chasing my dreams. I don't give up, I just divert. The goal is still there. I am still on my way to making it happen, just taking a different route.

I was at a yoga class recently and the teacher said, 'Don't go against the flow, go with it.' That made me think a lot. When you work hard you expect a specific outcome, usually you expect success. If this doesn't happen, what do you do? The normal reaction is to be upset, angry at someone who rejected you, disappointed with yourself and possibly ready to give up on your efforts. But what if you thought about it in a different way? What if you said, 'I am working really hard and the outcome of this can be 50 per cent one way (positive outcome) or 50 per cent another way (negative outcome).' It's the old glass half-empty, glass half-full difference in perspective. However, rather than thinking about it in a positive or negative way, why not just be thankful for the water? It's going with what you have. If outcome one happens, these will be my options and next steps; if outcome two happens, then these are my options and next steps. Go with the flow, float with the breeze. Rather than prepare yourself for just one result, prepare yourself for any and all possible outcomes and just follow different next steps and opportunities.

Another thing I learned on my rocky path was that it's not just the rejection that throws you off balance, it's also the highs and the lows. When everything around you is moving so fast and it's changing by the minute, how do you deal with that? Take a breath, keep calm and keep going.

November 2017. We just signed up Sofia Richie to do a campaign for NIP+FAB. Unlike some of the other deals we've signed with celebrities in the past, this one seemed to be going really smoothly. Her team of managers, agents, lawyers and publicists were very professional and so easy to work with, and were keeping us in the loop every step of the way, which in this business is rare. Naturally we were all super excited to work with her and bring some new blood to the NIP+FAB family, especially as this campaign would be the follow-up to our two successful campaigns with Kylie Jenner. Oddly enough, Sofia Richie was dating Scott Disick, ex-partner of Kourtney Kardashian, so in a weird way we were also keeping it with the Kardashian family.

We planned for Sofia to come to London and spend a day with us. We would be shooting, doing media interviews and then we would be hosting a Q&A for press and influencers.

We all arrived on a Tuesday morning at the Bulgari Hotel in London, where the shoot would take place. Sofia had travelled in with her agent from New York and booked a glam team in London. A lot of celebrities fly their glam teams with them but she was happy to work with a local team (always a bonus when you save on budgets). We arrived a bit earlier to prepare for the shoot and got a beautiful suite at the Bulgari with a bedroom, glam area, sitting room and dining room. We set up a corner for the shoot and prepared the lights. Sofia arrived on time, looking stunning. She was wearing a sexy pant suit by Elizabeth and James, and her hair and makeup were perfect. Sofia is very sweet and super nice and has a great sense of humour. It was refreshing to find that she does not take herself too seriously. Apart from her stunning looks, she immediately disarms you with her real tomboy attitude ... she is fantastic! The vibes were great on that day.

The whole NIP+FAB team was there as a campaign day tends to be really busy and you need all the help you can get. From directing the photographer, to making sure we get all the assets that we need for the brand, to ordering lunch for everyone – it's a full-on military-style operation. Everything is scheduled and precisely timed on a day like this, every second is precious. My phone was glowing red hot as I marshalled my troops through every aspect of the day and, as I liaised with Sofia's team on the schedule, the room was alive with activity in every corner.

It was about halfway through the shoot that I suddenly got a call from the office that our creative director had just resigned. I had to sit down. This was someone that had worked for me for many years. She was practically family. We worked day and night together to shape the creative direction of the business, we went on trips together, did hundreds of shoots and she was one of the people that not only I was counting on but thought would stay with me for years to come. The feeling of losing a valued member of the team is like losing family. Suddenly this glamorous shoot with Sofia Richie didn't matter any more. All I wanted to do was go back to the office and take care of business. Find out why. What happened. Was it because I asked her to change the background of yesterday's shoot from pale pink to dusty pink or because I asked her team to tidy up the studio? Did I offend her? I needed to get to the bottom of this, right then!

My stomach was constantly doing a 'flip' – a sort of combination of butterflies, vertigo and heart attack ... I'm pretty sure you have had it. I reminded myself to stay calm: all will be sorted. We were there to do a job and my HR problem could not get in the way of such an important day. Nevertheless, my eyes were on swivel mode every second, and every second that passed made me more tense. I didn't say anything, kept smiling and kept going with the shoot.

The second we got the last shot and Sofia was out of the suite I could let go of my calm pretence and actually panic out loud. I made my way back to the office and had that meeting with the creative director. I heard her out, tried to change her mind but her reasons of leaving were beyond my control. And sometimes you can't control everything. I could have left in the middle of the most important campaign of the year out of panic and still would have had the same result.

I had to keep it all together despite going quietly crazy. This was such an important day for me, my team and for NIP+FAB that whatever drama happened at the office, I had to just keep on going, focus on the moment and make it happen. Keeping calm is the most important thing you can do when there's a crisis. Panic doesn't help with anything and drama just drains your energy. Narrow your focus, cut out the noise and concentrate on what you need to do to get out of this situation. There are always challenges along the way and keeping a cool head is what will take you to the other side.

Life and business are always a mix of highs and lows … and my book tour was no different.

Early 2018, my book had already hit the bestseller list on Amazon and I had set up a series of book signings in the US. The tour kicked off with the Q&A hosted by the whip-smart and supercool Alexa Chung at the Crosby. It was thrilling to hear that we were oversubscribed, with over a hundred people showing up to what we had thought would be an intimate session of maybe 50. At the Q&A there was standing-room only. A book signing followed where I met so many amazing women and a few men who were inspired by my story and were excited to read my book. I could have spoken to each of them for hours, I was on a real high. What an amazing start to the tour. News travels fast and soon the dates we had planned in advance were being supplemented by lots of interviews and TV appearances.

This opening flurry of activity was followed by yet another signing in NY at the end of the week at the 'Simply Stylist' conference. Simply specialise in events where they bring together fashion, beauty and entrepreneurial leaders and pioneers to inspire and learn from one another. I opened the conference and did a book signing. Once again I was stunned. This time the line was so long that we ran out of books. People were coming to me asking me to sign my name on a card and take a selfie. I was on top of the world.

The US tour continued with a panel appearance at a high-profile lifestyle conference in LA with the best and brightest female entrepreneurs, creatives and icons sharing their tips and tricks about business and success. Kim Kardashian was closing the conference on that day.

My speaking slot was at 3pm alongside Aimee Song and actress Nina Dobrev. We talked about social media, all of us coming from a different point of view. It was a great talk, the audience were warm and attentive, it felt really good. Another winning day! Wrapping up the talk, I announced that I was going to sign books after the conference, 'Make sure you come and see me', and with that off I went, eager to meet and greet the good people of California.

Now, when I have previously been booked at a conference and intend to follow up with a book signing, the conference usually assigns a space with a table and my books with some branding in the background. They tend to have a lot of speakers at this kind of event so often have a whole 'signing area' with rope and posts to control the thronging crowds and a published timetable, good selfie lighting, security for when it gets crazy and paramedics for when it all gets too much for the admiring fans. All in a day's work for the jet-setting author of *How to Be an Overnight Success*. We usually sent someone the day before to check the set up and the space but we had such a busy week in LA that we just hadn't had the time to do the advance visit. However, this was a massive and very respected conference event; their website describes how 'attendees come together to feel inspired, enhance their business, mix, mingle and cultivate new friendships in an amazing and beautiful environment'. Sounded great. No worries there then.

I finished my panel and started making my way to where I had been told I was to do the book signing. I stood, slightly stunned, rather confused and definitely not impressed by what I was seeing. It was just an open space at the edge of the huge conference hall. There was no booth, no branding, no table. It was far from a designated signing area. It was

68

basically a Mexican canteen with rough outdoor-style wooden tables and benches.

OMG, I could die. In case you are wondering, a casual canteen with people eating tacos and enchiladas on the next table is not the ideal space for a book signing but, being the professional I am, I brushed the dried chilli-beans and encrusted guacamole from the table and set up my signing area. That was when we hit the next snag: since there was no designated place for book signings at this event, no one knew where to find me and so no one showed up. So there I sat, @MrsRodial, bestselling Amazon author, in my Balenciagas in the middle of a canteen surrounded by stacks of books. Yesterday I was in a glamorous New York hotel with queues out the door, today I am sat in a Mexican picnic with the pervasive aroma of refried beans and burritos in the air and not a soul waiting for me. I didn't know if I wanted to cry, laugh or eat a fajita.

My assistant started unboxing the books as if nothing was wrong and putting them in bags. She then started stopping everyone asking if they wanted a signed book from me (it's free!) and I think a few people pitied me and said 'OK, why not?' I was so embarrassed. Eventually, a couple of people showed up who had been at my talk and said how they loved my tips and were looking forward to reading the book but they hadn't known where to find me, so that gave me a bit of a boost. Sadly not many more managed to accidentally find me so I give my assistant the look. You know, the one that says, 'You deserve a large G&T and I need to get out of here.'

We took the books to the main conference area and just started giving them away, my philosophy being that if there wasn't going to be a signing at least people will get to read it. I definitely did not want to have to haul them back on to the plane home. In a glittering week of success and highs that was the lowest of the low and a moment I'd really like to forget ...

So who should I blame for this challenging experience? The conference organisers? My team? Myself? Mexican food? As always I have to blame myself. I took on so much during this trip, and eagerly said yes to every opportunity that came my way. I was excited to get out there and promote my book. I had a bad experience but this was also a lesson learned. Carried away by my new found fame as an author I took my eye off the ball. I should have looked at the resources more carefully, got more detail about the unique set up of the event and not assumed they would have the facilities. (Never assume – it makes an ASS of U and ME!) I should have paced myself and my team's time – better to do less but do it right.

So yes, I was so disappointed that my event wasn't successful but, at the same time, I'd had dozens of book signings with hundreds of readers showing up to share the love. I put myself out there with no guarantees of success, made the best of a really embarrassing situation and learned my lesson. And for the record, the conference itself was great and I do happen to like Mexican food.

One question I get asked a lot is, 'How do you deal with the highs and (especially) the lows of running a business?' It's a question that comes mostly from those wishing to start up – they tend to think that you only get highs and lows when you are starting up. This is a misconception. I have been running my business for years and while sometimes I feel that I am on top of the world, there are plenty of times when I feel completely defeated. There are times when I feel like I am killing it and times when I feel like that girl who was fired from banking and didn't know what to do with her life.

Life is unfair and business is unfair. I have been talking a lot about working hard and being passionate about what you do but, as you know, that's not all there is to it. I work 24/7 and I couldn't be more passionate about my company and my business. However, there are times when I question myself, times when I feel the world is not fair and everything is against me. Shit happens.

I've been in this business long enough to have seen brands and people come and go. One minute they are getting a lot of buzz and then suddenly they are no longer there, either gone bust or no one talks about them any more. I read an interview with Jay-Z a while ago and in it he revealed that the main reason for both his and his wife Beyoncé's success was that they didn't give up. This really says a lot and it speaks to me. You've had a bad day, it seems that the whole world is against you, you question yourself – it happens to all of us. Here is what you should do: just reset. Accept that you are having a bad day, get through it, don't block your feelings. Wake up the next day and use the energy of everything that went against you the day before to drive you to be the best that you can be today.

Strange as it may seem, I've had some of my best creative ideas after a bad day. After hitting a low, I go back to basics and think: *I am facing this problem, how do I get around this?* And I put together a plan of action to attack whatever is bothering me. The adversity I have faced somehow gives me extra energy. Will I solve the problem 100 per cent the next day? Most likely not, but I would take a few positive steps of action to take me where I want to be.

Make it Happen Secret #4

10 Tools to Deal with Rejection

I'd love to share with you my top ten tools for dealing with rejection in the best possible way and coming out the other end stronger and more confident. Use rejection as your motivator.

1. Take the time to digest the rejection and avoid any immediate knee-jerk actions and reactions. Haven't we all responded to a rejection email with anger and spite, breaking bridges and only regretting it when we are in a better state of mind? The first thing I do is try to calm down my nerves. I try to schedule a workout session when possible, do a mini meditation or call a friend for a mega gossip session. I try to move my emotions on from the rejection and focus my mind on something different. It's all a matter of perspective.

2. Say to yourself that it's not the end of the world. Most times we tend to exaggerate the importance of a rejection and make it much bigger in our minds than it actually is.

3. Shift your attention to someone else. Our ego is what makes us get mad and drives us to do crazy things when angry. Try to be nice to someone else. Do something nice for a loved one, or someone at your office, something unexpected, and show your appreciation. This would create positive feelings in both yourself and the other person and will make you feel much better about yourself.

72

4. Don't put yourself in the position of the victim. Especially for the first 48 hours, avoid any negative thoughts about yourself as this will only take you back. You are who you are, you are special, you know you are working hard to achieve your goals. Don't get into negative self-talk – who is that going to help?

5. Do something nice for yourself to make you feel better. I stop by a coffee shop that I haven't been to for a while, or listen to some uplifting music, or buy something nice that I've wanted to for a while, or go have a manicure, or repeat-watch my favourite TV show. Go to a high-vibe place, get a glass of champagne. Make yourself feel special. These are the times you need to treat yourself.

6. Talk to someone. A friend, a colleague, a relative. Just find someone who will listen to you and won't judge. You are not actively looking for solutions yet: you just need to get it all off your chest. Sharing your thoughts with someone you trust helps you process your frustration and sometimes find the resolution that you are looking for.

7. Focus on what you have in life. Write a list of the top ten things you are grateful for right now. Your health, family, recent achievements, people in your life that uplift you. Regardless of what happens to us, there are always some great things in our lives that we need to value. Be grateful for what you have rather than always focusing on what you don't have.

8. Reset. Every rejection is an opportunity to redefine your goals and plan of action. If plan A hasn't

worked out, it's not the end of the world. Come up with a plan B. The important thing is to keep on moving, keep progressing. One thing will lead to the next, and you are ultimately going to achieve your goal. You just have to keep going and be patient.

9. Don't think it's about you. I see this all the time when we interview people at work. We may see an amazing candidate but they may be too junior or too senior for a certain position. It's all about the fit and it has nothing to do with them. So don't blame yourself.

10. Always remember: when you have a bad day, there is always a great day waiting for you around the corner. We all have our good days and bad days. And statistically, if you work hard and keep a positive attitude, a great day *is* waiting for you around the corner.

5

Don't Let Anyone Work Harder Than You

So you've made the start, you've sent the first email, you've got that project started. What's next? The next step is hard work and determination. There are no shortcuts to success.

What does hard work mean? Hard work means that you put in the hours, you put in the effort, you put in the practice to be the best version of yourself: working hard to be the best that you can be. It's the idea of being not only the biggest fish in a small pond but the *best* fish in that pond. You don't need to be the best of the best, just be the best at whatever situation you are in or whatever small opportunity is given to you. Why settle on being average when you can be the best?

Let's take public speaking. My dream was always to speak at a *WWD* (*Women's Wear Daily*) conference. It's a very prestigious event that brings together a whole host of incredible people from the fashion, beauty and tech industries in one very inspiring day. With that mix of people in the room, you can imagine what a great place it was for me or indeed anyone to do a bit of quality networking and to tell their story. I had been going to that conference as an attendee for several years and had often sat in the forums listening to another amazing entrepreneurial story or fashion-insider gem thinking. As I scribbled notes in the dark, I would think how amazing it would be if one day I could be one of those speakers. You know me by now ... it wasn't that I was too shy to put myself forward, it's just not that easy to get a spot on that conference. I had an interesting story, I had things to say, so I ticked a certain amount of boxes, I guess, but this is a leading industry event. They want to know that you are going to really engage an audience, and can tell your story with passion and dynamism. Basically they want to be sure they get a bit of showbiz with the real biz. They want to see examples of you speaking at other events, but to be honest I was still a public-speaking newbie and wouldn't have had much to show them even if they asked.

Around the same time as I was dreaming of speaking at *WWD*, I was invited to speak at a much smaller conference in London. There were only about 50 attendees so I guess they were happy to take a chance on me … and being a smaller, more intimate event, it was a much more forgiving audience.

Sure, it wasn't my dream mega-conference, I didn't step out to thunderous applause, dazzling lights and my face on a 50-foot video screen, but it was a step on the road to that dream. So I prepared and rehearsed as though it were that dream event: I wanted to be the best I could be. I knew I wasn't going to be a ready-made Steve Jobs or Michelle Obama (both effortlessly charismatic speakers) at my first engagement, but I set out to make a great impression and to be the best speaker at that event. I wanted to be the person that provided the most value to the audience, the one that stood out. I wanted the audience to talk about my work and I wanted both my message and myself to be memorable.

On top of all of this, I had my eye on the future. I wanted to make sure I used this opportunity to build my experience and my reputation so that other conferences would want to book me, and I could share the stage with the sort of speakers I used to pay to see. I wanted to be the best on that small, starter conference because being the best creates bigger opportunities down the line, opportunities such as one day being asked to speak at *WWD*.

So how did I do? Well, I think I did OK. I didn't clear the room and most people stopped looking at their phones while I was speaking so I'm calling that a success. Was I the best? Well, the audience would have to be the judge of that. The point is that I strove to be the best and I got myself out

78

there and I did it. I practised hard but with the knowledge that, if it didn't go well, it wasn't the end of my career ... I made it out alive and had built up my experience. 'Life goal: spoke at a conference. Tick.'

Doing that first event gave me the confidence to take on the next one and the next one, each time learning what works, when to pause for effect while telling that story, when to look at the audience to draw them in, when to keep it light, when to be still and deliver a serious point. Like a stand-up comedian or an actor trying out their material, I was amazed at how small differences in the way I inflected or softened my voice at particular moments in a story could have huge effects on the way an audience responded to it. I was slowly improving my skills and getting better every time, but one thing remained constant. Every time, regardless of how big or small the conference was, I would always go prepared, notes at the ready, well-rehearsed, timed and focused on presenting myself in the best possible way. And yes, you won't be shocked to learn that this anecdote ends with my dream coming true just a few years later.

Yes, dear reader, I did speak at the *WWD* conference ... and it was amazing. But the important part of this is how I got there. I realised that goal by giving my best effort at every single opportunity that came my way, practising, learning, adapting and not being afraid to get out there.

You need to make the best of every situation and ensure you stand out. It doesn't mean you need to be the best in everything ... although that would be nice ... just find something that you can be amazing at and make people notice. Get people talking about how great you are, make a name for yourself. Create word-of-mouth on your greatness and more great things will come your way.

Sometimes these opportunities don't always seem obvious. There may be times when an opportunity comes to you but it's not 100 per cent what you want. I have a friend who wanted to be a showbiz editor and her first opportunity out of college was writing for a sports section of a newspaper. Was she into sports? No. Was this what she wanted to do with her life? Not at all. Did she take the opportunity? Yes she did! She put aside her ambivalence about people kicking and throwing things for entertainment and she did the best job she could do as a sports writer. As it happens, the newspaper also had a showbiz department and so while impressing the editors with her sports journalism, she started connecting with the right people in the showbiz department and when a position opened up, she was in an ideal position to get the job. It was still an entry-level role but she was on her way and working towards her goal. So the take away here is that she took the sports role, even though it wasn't her dream job, but despite this, she didn't half-ass it: she gave it her all, made her mark and built a great reputation at the paper, so when the opportunity she had been looking for arose she was top of the list. By being the best 'fish' in the sports pond she made the leap into the showbiz lake. She made it happen.

When I first started Rodial, a lot of retailers wouldn't want to commit to taking the full range. I was given the opportunity to launch just one product. Was it ideal? No. But that was a foot in the door of someone I wanted to do business with. I needed to work my butt off to make sure that product was a success so when they came to review it they would see the success and take a bigger range next time. Yes, it was hard graft and sometimes for little initial reward, but they gave my product exposure and recognition and legitimised my brand, and I concentrated on being the best supplier I could be to that store. I worked harder than I probably needed to but the pay-off was more orders and another step on the journey to growing Rodial.

So take any opportunity that comes your way and make the best of it. Grabbing an opportunity and taking action will keep you motivated, get you out there and give you a competitive advantage to everyone else, especially those people saying 'no' until they get the perfect one. I predict those people will be waiting a long time, because it rarely works that way. Say yes, stay positive, put your best foot forward and turn this small opportunity into your big break. It's all down to you.

As Malcolm Gladwell explains in his book *Outliers: The Story of Success*, you need 10,000 hours of practice to gain mastery of a skill. He argues that talent will never become an expertise without practice, lots of practice. He refers to studies that examined the practising habits of expert and amateur musicians and chess players. These studies found that no expert rose to the top without practice, and no amateur failed when they put in many hours of practice. He analyses the success of The Beatles as an example, who took the low-key opportunity to play in Hamburg, Germany, in 1960, and honed their skills in little clubs, playing long sets seven days a week, so that by the time they began having worldwide success in 1964, they had played approximately 1,200 live shows ... significantly more than most bands today ever play in their lifetimes. Gladwell argues that The Beatles were no doubt an example of great talent, but what set them apart was the hours that they put into their practice.

To be successful, to make it happen, you need to work harder and smarter than your competition. Successful people go out there and drive their progress; the rest are happy to coast, waiting for others to give them a development and education plan. I have always wanted to be in control of my life, career and success, and have always gone that extra mile, done the extra rep and put in the extra time to make it happen.

I get a lot of questions from new entrepreneurs and quite often the same frustrated question pops up: 'I work really hard but things aren't happening for me.'

I hear this again and again. First of all, working hard means different things to different people. I work at my office eight hours a day but on top of that I spend at least one hour in the morning and one hour in the evening reading, researching, educating myself. I use my mornings, evenings and weekends to progress projects that I don't have time to work on during the day: writing my book, preparing for a podcast recording or doing research on new fashion trends to put new looks together for the next season. Nine-to-five is my job and out of hours is my career.

Working hard means challenging yourself and always moving forward. If you are working hard and just doing the same thing over and over, there won't be much progress. You need to think outside the box, or even better climb out of the box and throw the box away, or recycle it into a bigger, better, greener box, or fashion the box into a range of cute accessories. Whatever you do, just get outside the box! Think differently. Spend some time considering what other skill you could benefit from learning. Ask yourself, *What other areas can I research into that would help me with my goals?* Get a new perspective and you may discover that eureka moment.

OK, back to the question. You say you're working hard but things aren't happening for you? What is your timeline? Things take time to happen, but as long as you are following your goal plan and are seeing some progress, then something is going right. You can't become a success overnight, right? (Drat, I told myself I wouldn't mention that again … oh well.) Have a realistic timeline and your hard work *will* pay off. Success is not a sprint, it's a marathon. There is very little that can be achieved from one day to another but a lot that can be achieved over two years. Remember, incremental gains are still moving you towards winning that gold medal.

Let's define hard work. Sometimes it's the sheer amount of time that you put into driving your own success and sometimes it's the mental strength to overcome challenges. Very often, I put in the hours, do my research, think outside the box and still don't get the result that I worked for. This is where the hustle begins ... and hustle *is* hard work. When you've been rejected time after time, you take stock of the rejection, shape yourself up and go at it again. I see a lot of entrepreneurs giving up at this point, not because they haven't progressed but because they've been rejected a few times and decide to quit. The good news is that you can train your mind to take on those challenges, process them and then move on (ask any jobbing actor about 'learning to love no' – they face it in auditions every day). For me the mental intensity that happens when you drive your own destiny is the hardest part. It's hustle all the way.

I remember when I first met Mario Dedivanovic, Kim Kardashian's makeup artist. I had a lot of respect for him and for his work. He had supported us with Rodial and NIP+FAB a few times but I'd yet to meet him face-to-face and so when the timetables finally aligned we arranged to meet in New York. We met for drinks at the very splendid Soho Grand Hotel and I soon got him talking about how he started his career as a makeup artist with Sephora. Wow, what a journey and (pause for effect) it was an overnight success that took him almost eighteen years (the overnight success magic number it seems!). These days he's the makeup artist of one of the most well-known celebrities in the world, he's hosting his own masterclasses (good luck getting on the waiting list for one of those!) and he has fans everywhere.

Time flew by and I was loving our chat, so I asked him if he could stay for dinner. He explained that he'd love to but just couldn't. 'I have a shoot tomorrow,' he said. I thought he meant he had to be up for an early morning shoot with some mega-celebrity and so needed to have an early night. 'No,' he said, 'I am shooting a beauty story for an online magazine on lip shades that go with different skin colours, and need to spend the rest of my evening doing my research and planning for the shoot.'

I immediately saw why and how he had reached the top of his game. You would think a celebrity makeup artist with eighteen years' experience would rest on his laurels and just do what he always does. Not him. He was up late doing his research and making sure he would be the best that he could be.

This is the sign of a successful person, always striving to do your best, always re-inventing yourself and always keeping ahead of the game.

We live in a world where everything moves so fast, sometimes you need to run just to keep up, otherwise, as Heidi Klum points out each week on *Project Runway*: 'One day you are in, the next day you are out.'

But hard work isn't just about hours and effort: it's about evolving, responding and learning. It's about constant reinvention. Something that happens to all of us, whether we own a business that has been around for a while, we're a freelancer working for ourselves or we work for a company and have been doing the same job for a few years, is that we will start to see new people cropping up in our industry or our company. They are annoyingly young, energetic and restless, with a lot of new ideas and spark. So where do we stand?

To succeed, we need to keep moving, we need to keep learning and we need to keep innovating. Think about Madonna and how she has been reinventing herself album after album. New look, new hair, new music, always current, always cool, always making people notice.

So keep on reinventing yourself, keep innovating and keep moving forward ... never stay still.

One way to keep your inspiration is to constantly look at yourself and your product and think, *Am I or the product still relevant? Am I up to speed with the new trends?* Every now and then you need to take a step back and assess where you can be doing better. It's hard, as this process makes you realise your weaknesses and it's painful to admit them, but it has to be done to evolve yourself and your brand. It's also hard because you live inside your own bubble ... it's difficult to stand outside and give an assessment that might be useful. I mean, how would a fish describe water? So pool some opinions, take on board some criticism, ask for opinions. They will all help to get a better picture of how people see you and your business, and help you hit the right targets when it comes to making changes.

Reinventing yourself will keep your business moving in the right direction, or at least taking the first steps in that direction if things have started to slow down or stand still. Just because everything is working out fine for you right now doesn't mean things will always stay the same. Make the changes before you have to; keep ahead of the race. You change, competition changes, new trends come and go. To continue being successful you need to adjust. You need to take a hard look at yourself and decide what stays and what goes.

Make it Happen Secret #5

10 Tips to Fire You Up You When You Don't Feel Like Working Hard

1. Connect yourself with new people. We always draw energy from those around us. Get out there and connect with new people in your industry. Get a new perspective and move to a circle of people with positive and exciting energy who represent your future and not your past. Often, people from our past hold us back. You need to break free. You are the average of the five people that you hang out with the most. So pick carefully who you spend your time with.

2. Read one hour a day. Reading is the quickest way to success. If one hour is too long, start with 20 minutes and do it for a couple of weeks to develop a habit. The most successful people in the world (Bill Gates, Elon Musk) attribute their success to reading.

3. Keep on learning. Subscribe to some new industry newsletters, read some new industry magazines, find some new podcasts, read the weekend newspapers. Attend talks, conferences and any opportunities in your industry. Promise to learn something new every single day.

4. Find a mentor. I get asked a lot if I had a mentor when I started my business. And when I say no, they look at me in disbelief. Did you do all this *without* a mentor? I never had a direct mentor, but I did have a lot of

indirect mentors. These are people that I admire and I read everything about them. Biographies, books, articles. Mentors can be authors that you admire and they mentor you through their books. Don't fall into the trap of saying, 'I really want to be successful but I heard I need to get a mentor and no one will take me!' Babes, we are the 'make it happen' team, we don't have time for excuses! There are lots of indirect mentors out there: find someone you can relate to and get all the material on them, and hey presto, here is your mentor!

5. Rewrite or edit your to-do list. When was the last time you took a hard look at your to-do list? Split it into three: 1. things that can be done within 24 hours; 2. things that can be done within a week; 3. things that can be done within three months. There may be things that aren't relevant any more, you may have already completed them or your goals may have changed. Keep it fresh and current.

6. Reward yourself when you finish a challenging piece of work. It could be anything from going to a new restaurant, to having a bubble bath that evening, to buying a new accessory.

7. Declutter your workspace. Go through all paperwork and get rid of what you don't need any more, recycle, delete old emails and organise your folders, refresh your pen holder and get some coloured pens and pencils, clean and tidy your desk and cabinet. Your workspace will feel inviting and ready for action.

8. Listen to your favourite music. Anything that makes you feel happy, uplifted and creative.

9. Brainstorm ideas for a project that you are excited about. Make a list of whatever comes into your mind. Process and organise later.
10. Celebrate your wins. Even if they are small ones. Don't discount the little things: acknowledge every small step and progress even if it wasn't done perfectly. How often do you discount a small win just because it wasn't done perfectly? Always be positive about your small successes. You need more wins in your life to motivate, encourage and help you see how amazing you really are.

6

Your 6am
Wake-Up
Call to
Success

London, March 2005. I had just moved into a new office at Rodial. Work was crazy (as always). Each day, I worked non-stop in the office, then at home I continued to do more work and I would finally finish my day at 10pm. I would then turn on the TV and start watching anything, really, to take my mind off work. I would watch for two, three, four hours and go to bed after midnight. The next day my alarm would go off at 8am. I would wake up grumpy, rush to have a shower and get ready for work. No time for breakfast, I stopped by a Starbucks close to work and picked up a Venti Cappuccino and a pastry. At my desk by 9am, cappuccino and breakfast in hand, ready to get on with my day. It was a very stressful time at work. We had just moved to bigger offices and hired some new people, and the expenses were going through the roof. I was like a zombie going from work to home and home to work in a constant state of anxiety and feeling that I was always running out of time. I was miserable. Something had to change.

I started analysing my day. I was getting frazzled from rushing into my morning, dealing with traffic, getting in line at Starbucks to get my breakfast at the busiest time of the day and arriving at work rushed and wondering how to motivate myself today, while going through the non-stop emails and team meetings. I felt that I was always having to be very reactive, I was in a defensive position, waiting for things to come at me rather than proactively driving my day.

Somewhere I found the time to read an article on the benefits of waking up early. It said that people who wake up earlier get a lot more done in their day. While the rest of us use the snooze button, they are out there training for marathons, planning their career and taking the steps needed to make it happen for themselves.

Apple CEO Tim Cook wakes up at 3.45am, does his emails for an hour, then goes to the gym, then Starbucks (for more emails), then work. Michelle Obama starts her days with a 4.30am workout before her kids wake up. Twitter co-founder Jack Dorsey wakes up at 5.30am to meditate and go for a six-mile jog. Anna Wintour plays tennis each morning at 5.45am. Then she has her hair and makeup professionally done before she goes to the office (and has it done again for the evening). Oprah wakes up at exactly 6.02am (not 6.01 and definitely not 6.03). Her first thought of the day is 'Oh, I'm alive. Thank you!' At 6.45am she drinks a chai tea or skinny cappuccino before she goes to the gym, then she meditates. Victoria Beckham wakes up at 6am and does an hour at the gym before the kids wake up, then gives them breakfast, and then she fits in another hour of workout before she goes to work. Kim Kardashian works out at 6am for an hour and a half.

But the morning routine that blew me away was that of Mark Wahlberg, the Hollywood actor who has made over 50 movies and is reported to be worth £175 million. He posted his daily routine on Instagram and it went viral. He gets up at 2.30am to pray at 2.45am followed by a 3.15am breakfast of oats, peanut butter, blueberries and eggs. He then prepares to go to his private gym to work out. After a 95-minute workout, he goes on a 7½-mile uphill hike, then prepares a sheep's milk smoothie, showers, plays golf, and jumps in a minus 150°C cryotherapy chamber. All this before I used to be in the queue at Starbucks. And if that wasn't enough, he later finds time to post another video from his gym with this pep talk: 'Do I work hard because I am in this position? No, I got to this position because I work harder than everyone else.'

I am already exhausted by the mere thought of what all these successful people achieve while the rest of us are still asleep. We don't need to go to these sort of extremes, and I would say that waking up at 3.45 is neither advisable nor feasible for most of us: for a start we do need to have sufficient sleep to be able to function the next day. The valuable nugget within these tales of celebrity extremes is that getting a head start in the morning, being proactive with that time and using the first more productive hours well can help set the tone for the rest of your day.

So, always one for self-improvement and undeterred by the fact that I don't have my own cryotherapy chamber to hand, I decided to give this waking up early thing myself a go. I took a deep breath, set my alarm at 6am and started my experiment by simply giving myself some more time to wake up and ease into my day. I have to admit, it wasn't easy to break my sleep pattern at first but after grimly setting the alarm for a few days in a row, it did become easier. I started going to bed a bit earlier and after a while it felt less like I was rising from a shallow grave and more like I had actually had a refreshing night's sleep ... I even started to beat the alarm on some mornings. And OMG! I had a *whole extra hour* in the morning to get a start on my day. Time to catch up on the news, read a book, meditate, even fit in a gym session. Things started changing. I was calmer, I arrived at work more grounded and had a sense of purpose for the day. Those early morning hours are a time of the day when no one wants my attention and I can fully focus on positive and creative me-time. The phone does not ring, the email does not ping, and I can do my thing.

Now I look back on the lack of a morning routine and I see it made me think I had no time. It was causing me to waste my working day in unimportant activities and I had no sense of achievement at the end of it. Wasting my morning energy and starting my day on the wrong foot wasn't helping me achieve my goals or chase my dreams. Now I had a routine I could really see the positive changes. I developed a little ritual. To start my day I have a glass

93

of hot water and lemon followed by an organic double espresso. Coffee in hand, I plan my day, learn something new, meditate and fit in a workout session. My day already looks well spent.

Early mornings can be your golden hours. Using mornings well is what separates successful from unsuccessful people. Waking up at 6am or earlier, successful people have already worked out, bettered themselves and are taking the steps to achieve the lives they want to live. Successful people have things they want to achieve, they have plans to make and dreams to dream and those early mornings are the times when they have most control of their schedules. Successful people use this time to hear the small voice inside themselves, to allow thoughts to flow unchallenged, to self-motivate – to clear the decks, make space and prepare for the next big thing. If you wait until the end of the day to do important but not urgent activities such as working out, meditation, reading, planning your business or career, it will most likely not happen.

It all has to do with willpower. Research has shown that we have the most willpower at the beginning of the day. Willpower is like a muscle that can tire from being overused. As we get on with our day, dealing with challenges from traffic, frustrating colleagues or sticking to our diet, our supply of willpower is used up fast. I have noticed how I tend to lose self-control towards the end of the day. Studies have shown that the majority of impulse crimes are committed after 11pm: drug use, alcohol abuse, gambling and similar situations tend to happen later in the day. It's something I still fight myself, having managed to eat healthily all day, I tend to indulge in sweet treats at night. Usually, I am not even hungry, I just need that sweet boost after I have resisted it all through the trials and tribulations of another busy working day.

Going back to the early start, the reason that those hours are so important is that at those times we have the willpower and energy to tackle things that require internal motivation, things that might not be urgent or necessary but nonetheless are things that, if we do them, will lead us to success. The great thing about willpower is that if you use it to develop helpful early morning rituals and you do them often enough, they will become habits. The minute you develop those habits, they stop taking so much energy and they don't even require that much willpower. Successful people turn those high-willpower tasks into rituals so their energy can be used to deal with the annoying things that inevitably pop up later in the day, such as late trains, frustrating colleagues or slow internet, that will drive you crazy and make you want to eat the whole box of chocolate-chip cookies. (Yes, that is a confession ... and yes, it has happened more than once.) But I suppose by developing those rituals and getting that gym session out of the way first thing you've already burned the calories and can indulge later. (Actually, I just realised this as I am writing it ... I am going to treat myself to some choc-chip cookies right now!)

(PAUSE FOR COOKIE.)

'OK,' you say to me, 'I already wake up early, where is my Rolls-Royce?' But ask yourself what you are using that time for? I love checking my social media, and could easily be on Instagram for two hours in the morning, and it is also the perfect moment to catch up on a couple of boxset episodes. Well, that would be a waste of time, or at least a waste of time for the sort of person that wants to make it happen. You need to use that precious and most productive time to do things to improve your career/business/life and ultimately achieve success. If your job revolves around social media or you are a TV executive and need to check out a new series for work then by all means be on Instagram or watch TV first thing … but for the rest of you mornings are for other activities! These need internal motivation and will help set the tone for your day. If followed regularly, they will lead you to success.

This is my personal list of 'things that I like to practise in the morning'. Sometimes I do all of them, sometimes just a few, depending on the morning and my priorities for the day:

Working on Personal Development

Mornings are your ideal time for personal development. During the day, you have a job. In the early morning, you have a career. For me this is one of the most exciting parts of my day. I catch up with industry news, research a new project, read a few pages from an inspirational book or listen to a podcast. This is the time that I am uninterrupted by work or family and can focus on developing myself and my skills. This is the time that I invest in myself to take me forward to my career.

Personal development doesn't happen overnight. It starts with baby steps and builds to giant strides, but there's a lot of shoe-leather being worn down in the meantime. Every morning, take three small steps towards your goal, whatever that goal may be, personal or professional. They could be as small as sending an email or making a call or putting five minutes aside to complete a difficult task. Do these small steps every day and you will see how these will amount to huge leaps in your personal growth over the years. Already, by reading this book, you are a step ahead of the game. You are already finding ways to motivate yourself, get ideas, research and take the steps you will need to help achieve your dreams. And I hope that rather than postponing reading this book until you have a big chunk of time, you are reading a chapter in the morning.

Making a Plan for the Day

Another thing I like to do in the early morning is plan my day. I am too tired to do it the night before. I like to look at my schedule with fresh eyes and get excited about the upcoming meetings and opportunities of the day. I visualise every meeting and make some notes on the purpose of the meeting and what we want to achieve, so I have a clear direction for every meeting.

This is the time when I come up with tons of ideas for work and my team. It could be a new product, a new design inspiration, a new press event or even a solution to a work challenge. I type the emails and keep them on draft until about 8.30 as I don't want my team to wake up (unless it's super urgent) and panic. When they start their day they will have my ideas and will be ready to go!

Working Out

I know that unless I work out first thing in the morning, I won't work out at all. Before I had a morning routine, I would work all day, with every intention of going home, changing into workout gear and making it to the gym that evening. Well, guess what? It never happened. There would always be excuses, and some good ones too! 'I am too tired from work'; 'I had a long day'; 'It's been a crazy day,

I don't have the mental capacity to focus on working out'; 'I need to be around to respond to work emails'; 'I have an event to attend'; 'I need to spend more time with the kids'; 'It's raining'; 'I don't feel like walking to the gym' – so many excuses, so little muscle tone.

I also realised that I wasn't the one to go to the gym and plan my own workout. In fact, that was one of the major things holding me back: I not only had to drag myself to the gym, but when I got there I had to think of what to do. So, to avoid this I started by working out with a trainer. Suddenly I had a 7am slot booked in the diary and I just had to show up ... no excuses. When you make that appointment, you just have to set the alarm and you have to show up. It's just too easy to find an excuse to duck out if you are working out alone; it's a lot harder to let someone else down, and besides, those sessions are non-refundable so you may as well drag yourself there and get your money's worth.

After a few months of personal training I was aware that it was getting a bit expensive and, besides, I felt I needed a bit of variety, so I started looking for some early morning classes in my neighbourhood. I tried a few things and finally identified some classes that I liked, walking distance from home (it has to be under 15-minute walk to make it easy), and you can book them like appointments. I now know that Monday/Wednesday/Friday at 7am I am doing a class and everything revolves around it. I try to avoid early morning meetings on those days, and instead schedule those on Tuesday and Thursdays. If I have to schedule an early morning meeting, I move to a 6am class. If I need to do a one-day trip, I also schedule those on Tuesdays and Thursdays so as not to disrupt my workout days, or if I need to travel for a week, I get my team to check if there is a gym at my hotel or, if it's a big city, I research studios and classes that I can take while I am there.

It is part of my routine, so when I wake up early in the morning knowing that I have this class booked, I don't even think about it. All I need to do is wear my workout clothes, walk to the studio and, once I am there, I will make it happen. Being early in the morning, my willpower is fresh, working out is a ritual and I don't even think about how hard the class will be or if I will be able to finish it. I just show up not thinking about anything. All very zen, I suppose. Of course, it helps if you enjoy the class, the studio is cool and the instructor is motivating. The music is important too. In fact, sometimes I go to a class just because I like the music. Whatever the reasons, when I finish, I feel energised, motivated and ready to take the day. This is the time when I don't think about anything else … the world may be on fire outside for all I care. I just focus on the class, getting through lifting those weights and following the instructions. That focus really frees my mind, so if anything gets in the way of that it really puts a kink in my day now.

One time I was at Barry's Bootcamp and the woman on the bench next to me had her mobile on. Notifications were popping up, lighting up the screen constantly, and she repeatedly stopped working out and checked her phone. It was really distracting me. I never have my phone around while I'm at the gym: this is my time to totally switch off. Eventually I had to ask her to put her phone upside down as it was distracting. At the end of the class I had two people come and thank me for doing so.

Meditating

Meditation is a great way to start your day. Meditation makes you grounded, makes you calm and gets you ready to face the day's challenges with clarity. If you are in a frantic state of mind and a challenge comes up, you will react in a frantic way. If you are in a grounded state of mind and a challenge comes up, you will react to it with perspective, a calm approach and with a positive outlook.

Do I meditate every day? I used to. I now find that fitness is my meditation. But there are times when I feel overwhelmed with work, life and all sorts of challenges coming my way at the same time – it is at those times that I turn to meditation. I know there are people who take their meditation seriously and can sit down in silence for an hour. I am not like that. I need someone to tell me what to do, I need to follow a plan. There are tons of apps out there with all sorts of meditations, from a one-minute express meltdown meditation to half-hour advanced sessions. I personally love the 'Headspace' app, which I have on my phone. With it you can choose different packages based on the challenges that you are facing from work, relationships, health, creativity, whatever. You pick a package, choose the length of time you have to meditate and voilà!

When you meditate you become more creative. I've had team challenges that seemed impossible and, after meditating, I would come up with a solution, or I was stuck on a product idea and meditation showed me the way. All sorts of exciting things can come your way from meditating. As I am writing this, I am reminding myself I need to meditate more.

Still not convinced that taking a few minutes in the morning meditating is worth your while? Research has shown that meditation can help you in the following ways:

Meditation reduces stress. If you are a hustler, like me, stress is coming your way on a daily basis. When you hustle and you put yourself out there, you'll be dealing with the 'waiting game' or 'rejection', and you are constantly putting yourself in new and uncomfortable situations in order to progress. All these create stress. By meditating, you can find ways to control your emotions, so while you won't be able to remove the stressful situations from your life, you will be able to handle them in a cool and collected way. And that's a win.

Meditation improves concentration. How many times have you thought to yourself, *I have so many things to do, I don't know where to start*, or *I have so many ideas, I'm overwhelmed*, or your to-do list is endless. There is so much going on, you want to progress but you can't. You procrastinate. Meditation helps with focus, concentration and memory. There are times when everything is going crazy around me, dealing with work deadlines, team issues, requests for my time, family priorities and a million other things and it can get too much. In those moments of confusion, a good meditation session just magically shows me the way: where to start and how to prioritise. Give it a go.

Meditation helps improve relationships. Yes, you better believe it! In my pre-meditation days, any time I would be the target of a heated argument, an annoyed customer, a disgruntled employee or a stubborn child, I would go full-on into mirroring their emotions and getting into a battle with the aim to win. In the end, nothing would get resolved, I would be angry or resentful and nobody was happy. Meditation taught me to consider the other person's point of view and situation alongside mine and rather than going into an interaction with the aim of winning, I would go into it with an objective point of view and try to resolve the issue. Meditation helped me to remove my ego from every situation, to just be fair and maintain a positive relationship at the end of the dispute. Maybe that customer *is* right, maybe that employee has a valid point to consider, maybe my child needs to be

101

heard rather than being dismissed. I am not saying that in all cases you need to give in but I find that when I am in a grounded state of mind (after meditation) I tend to be more objective on my interactions.

I remember when I was trying to get my products into a new store and would get an email back saying they were not ready to work with us, and I could have been rude and defensive and acting from my ego. This was a major mistake as it would close the door on working with that store for ever. Now I would instead keep it positive and say, 'Thank you for your response, I appreciate your feedback, let's be in touch in the future', and keep that door open. It's just good karma.

Now, let's just be honest. I do get an extra one to two hours in the morning by waking up early but it doesn't mean I do it all: work out *and* meditate *and* work on my personal development *and* organise my day. There are days that I know I will work out, days I give to personal development, days for organising my plans for the day/week, and those for working on a creative project of mine. How do I decide? Well, some of it is going with the flow. For instance, when I was writing this book, some mornings I would wake up and be super inspired to write, so that's what I would focus my morning routine on. So set your plans but also listen to your instinct and give priority to what feels right (apart from pressing the snooze button).

Make it Happen Secret #6

10 Steps to Develop a Morning Routine

1. Start by setting your alarm 30 minutes earlier than your usual wake-up time. Get used to the new time and a few days later set it another 30 minutes earlier. Keep on doing this until you reach your ideal wake-up time.
2. Work out your ideal wake-up time. Everyone is different but the usual morning routine takes one to two hours.
3. While you are setting up your morning routine, develop an evening routine. You need to make up for the extra time that you gain in the morning by losing it from the evening.
4. You need to be away from your phone for at least 30 minutes (ideally an hour) before you go to bed for a good night's sleep.
5. Get an actual alarm clock to avoid having your phone next to you during the night. If you do need to have your phone next to you, turn off wifi and put it in airplane mode. To help yourself settle, have a warm bath, read a relaxing book or have some lavender tea. Find out what relaxes you. The quicker you get to sleep, and the better the quality, the more productive your morning routine will be.
6. Decide if your morning routine will involve any workout sessions and book them in your diary like meetings. Book all your classes on a Sunday and you're all set for the week.

7. Have a stack of inspiring books and magazines ready to be read. You need your material ready to go.
8. I like to make a hot water with lemon and an organic espresso. Find what you like and have it ready to go in the morning. Get a fun or cool mug/coffee cup or anything that makes your drink interesting.
9. Get a supply of coloured pencils. When I read a good book I like to underline the best parts or quotes and revisit them again.
10. When you are jet lagged, get back to your routine as soon as possible. I may sleep in the first day after a trip but on day two my alarm goes as normal. Breaking the routine for more than a few days will take you back a few steps.

7

Pay the Cost of Being the Boss

I am in the middle of a big retailer presentation and get a phone call from school. My kids didn't bring their sports kit and someone needs to urgently get it to them. Hubby responded that he can do it, thank God. He's a life saver. Presentation done and on my way to a shoot with an A-list celebrity. Son calls crying that his brother scored more goals at a football game and he is in hysterics. Keep calm, I will be back home soon. Let's get through this shoot and rush back home to sort out the football drama. Made it on time for dinner. Homework time but no one wants to do it. There's crying and screaming. Let's negotiate this. Trying to explain why homework needs to be done. Getting nowhere. Some bribing does it. Whatever it takes. Son reminds me we need to bake cupcakes for the school stall tomorrow to raise Monday for the 'Orangutans in Danger' charity. I certainly won't bake any cupcakes and who the hell knew orangutans were in danger anyway? Let's buy them from a store in the morning. Adding to my to-do list. Why can't I just write the school a cheque for £100 and have done with it? I can already see all the other perfect kids will be bringing elaborate home-baked cupcakes and my poor kid will show up with a value pack of Marks & Spencer cupcakes. Am I a bad mum?

Work and family, family and work, how do you hold it all together? There are so many roles to fill – entrepreneur, manager, counsellor, mentor, babysitter, cook, teacher, driver, nurse, housekeeper, stylist, mediator – you must become the very definition of a multi-tasker. I am pulled in so many directions every minute of the day that I have trained myself to do multiple things at the same time. Ordering online groceries on my way to a work meeting. Overseeing homework while taking a conference call. Responding to emails at a school function. There are so many demands on my time and attention that it's overwhelming and it's stressful but I just have to make it work.

107

I grew up in a working household. Both my parents worked. They worked mornings, evenings and weekends as they wanted to create a better future for me and my sister. My grandparents lived with us and helped raise us while my parents were working these long, punishing hours. From a very young age my parents instilled in me the value of being independent, always making my own money and being able to support myself. The way I was raised, I always saw myself as a working woman first and foremost: everything else was secondary. As soon as I was 18 I found a freelance job as a beauty writer at *Seventeen* magazine and was able to support myself in my studies ... and have supported myself ever since. Being financially independent is what I grew up to be and what I believed in. I saw my mum have a career and kids; she never stopped working while she had us and that was exactly what I was going to do. I wanted nice things in life and I was prepared to put in the work and extra hours to achieve my dreams.

Two years after starting the business, I had my first son. Then, two years later, I had my second. You will be unsurprised to learn that life and work suddenly became much more complicated and much more busy, although the baby bump was pretty useful for resting my laptop on. I really never stopped working, even right up to the last minute of pregnancy. I am slightly amazed at myself now, but even when I was in the delivery room I was managing to read and respond to my emails between contractions. Press send, gas and air, breathe, breathe! Repeat. I admit, I did take it easy during the first month after each of the births, but by the end of the first week at home I was doing a few store visits.

In my days in investment banking in New York, just before I started my own business, I was very impressed with some of the most successful female investment bankers

108

who returned to their jobs a month after they had a baby. We had special sessions where some of the more senior women would come in to tell us how they managed to return to work immediately after having their baby; they were living proof that you *can* have a career and a family. I really admired those women and they became my early career role models. They made me feel empowered and that I could be anyone I wanted to be.

Am I advocating this for everyone? No, I am not. I worked through pregnancy, childbirth and motherhood in my way ... it was the only way I knew, and I was comfortable with it. It worked for me and that is all: whatever works for you is the right thing to do, whether that is taking a year's maternity or leaving your career until your children are at school. There is no wrong answer ... I'm just sharing my story.

If there is one thing I have learned it's that there is no perfect time to start a family or start a business other than when it happens. Then, just roll with whatever comes your way. However and whenever you do it, I can tell you that it's not easy to combine the two, regardless of what the 'How does she do it?' features might indicate, and I certainly don't have it perfect. I seem to be in a constant state of mother's guilt, especially on the rare occasion when I do get time to do the school run and I see the other seemingly perfect mums dropping off and picking up their perfect kids. I naturally envisage a scene at their breakfast tables of perfect eggs and toast racks, of shoes shined and organic lunches lovingly prepared, the homework Mummy helped with the night before safely tucked in a coloured binder, hair combed, ties straightened, kiss on both cheeks, always there for a cuddle, a question or a crisis. Cut to the scene at our house: Mum left for work an hour ago, the kids are getting their own cereal, going to school on the bus with half a sports kit and their homework timetable is a mystery to me ... somehow it seems to get done.

But hold on, who's to say which way is better? Yes, Peter and Sally Perfect have a hands-on mum who is constantly there for them, but my kids have a mum who is showing them to be independent and to think and plan for themselves. I don't know the answer and I wouldn't presume to tell you a 'right way'. The reality is that I have a family that I love and a business that I am passionate about. And I want to make it work for both. I know it won't be perfect but I will do the best I can to keep all the balls in the air. There are great days when everything works like clockwork and I'm juggling like a star turn at the Palladium, and then there are other days when the whole thing comes crashing down. It's never perfect, and even if it seems perfect momentarily, it doesn't usually last. It's always a struggle and I have just learned to live with it.

So, we know that life gets far more complicated when you grow with your career or run a business and have kids, but there are ways to make it work. The key is to know what your priorities are. If all you want to do is spend every minute of the day with your family and raise your kids, then working full-time or having your own business would be very challenging. A business or a career is a living organism that needs all your attention. It's hard to run a business and grow it successfully or progress in your career on a part-time basis. It's not impossible, it's just harder.

If you want to focus on your business and career you need a support network around you. It could be your partner – after all, you do kind of co-own the kids – or your family or in-laws can be a real help if they live nearby, especially grans and grandads. However, make sure you consider the family politics. You need to share out the babysitting evenly between grannies. Woe betide you if you favour one granny over another! Friends can be useful, but again, make sure you offer reciprocal help and favours and look after/take out their kids too. You don't want resentment, and you want them to be there for you last minute if you need them. Then of course there is the nursery/day-care/school – if you are just getting started then you can squeeze a lot into the hours you get once the kids are at nursery, but ensure you plan your time/calls/calendar to fit in ... don't waste that precious time! And finally, if you have none of the above options you may need a nanny or housekeeper to help carry the load. They don't have to be an extravagance, and a nanny or childminder a couple of days a week can be perfect.

Whatever arrangement or timetable you come up with, you just need to accept that it's OK to delegate. And you need to trust these people. I know it's hard. When you haven't done this before, you think that no one else will love your kids the way that you do and that they will grow up to be horrible humans without you. And all you can think about is disaster ... you will find yourself agonising over every potential scenario from your child being left behind in the supermarket to you accidently booking a serial psycho killer as your babysitter. That feeling never ends – it's a life sentence. You'll still be worrying about that stuff when your kids have gone through university and are seemingly more mature and capable than you. That's being a parent. However, you can help yourself by calming the rising voice of paranoia, trusting others and letting go a bit ... and little by little the task of juggling work and family will become manageable.

And you know what? My kids spent time with all of the above in some capacity and I have to say they developed fine (I reserve the right to change this opinion when they become drug dealers or go on *Love Island*). They've had

111

fun times with nannies who had the energy to take them out to the park, when I didn't, and there was a housekeeper for a while who cooked them better meals than I ever would. I am eternally thankful for the grandparents we were lucky enough to have nearby who entertained them on school holidays and the day-care centres where they met and made a lot of new friends. It's my belief that living this latch-key life they engaged with a lot more people and became a lot more independent than if they spent all their living hours with me. While I am not there at every school event, I have learned to consider them in my plans: I pick the key ones to be there with them, an award, a sports day or even an 'Orangutans in Danger' cupcake-stall charity day, if that's where they want me to be.

I have realised that this sounds like I don't see my kids that much, but there are of course weekends and family holidays. Weekends are sacred. I work every living hour of the day and night in my business and career and I am mentally there all week. But at the weekend and on holidays (while still keeping an eye on emails), I do my best to spend quality time with them. We have all our meals together, play card games, go to a family movie ... it's family time all the time. When I was younger I used to go out a lot and meet friends all weekend. I don't do that any more: weekends are for family. I don't remember the last time I went out on a Saturday night partying. For real.

Remember, kids have their own interests too. One day I went back home, and both boys came back from school and sports visibly tired. I was tired too. 'Do you want to talk?' I asked them, hoping they wanted to talk to me about their day. 'No,' they said. 'Well, neither do I!' And we all got on our iPads and happily co-existed without putting in a forced effort. Don't assume kids needs to be entertained by you all the time. You can all be together in one room with everyone doing their own thing and that's all you need.

You may choose to work part-time or set up a business and go at a slower rate while raising a family. You can definitely do this and everything is possible. You need to do things your own way, with your own time. I am in no way an expert: I can't emphasise enough that you need to do what feels right for you. I am just here to tell you how I did it and, with every mother's challenges and frustrations, that yes, you can manage it all. It's not going to be perfect, but you can do it.

One of the challenges that I still face is when I have a tough day at work and go straight home. My mind is still wrapped around that work issue and not in the state of mind to be a mum when I go back home. I am physically there but my mind is loaded with all the work challenges and all I feel like doing is lying on the sofa and watching a boxset, but there are family things to do. Dinner to cook, school forms to be signed, kit to be washed, etc., etc. It feels like I am doing two jobs. I try to find a little pocket of time between work and home: it could be walking around the block a couple of times before I get back home and listening to a few minutes of a new playlist or podcast, or calling a friend or checking a favourite online magazine. I try to find a few minutes to do something that is neither work nor family related and that can give me a few minutes to myself and help me switch gears. Time to decompress from one thing and gear up for the next.

The key for me is a supportive partner who understands that there will be shortcuts in your life. That you won't be able to cook and serve elaborate dinners every evening, that your home may not always be in a perfect state and you may need some external help for household chores.

Your partner will need to step in and help out with the kids when you are not available. Before you decide to have a family and still pursue your career, it is crucial to have a conversation with your partner to make sure you will have that support and you will all be on the same page when you will be juggling both. If you are doing this on your own then first of all, 'GO YOU!'; second of all, you will really need to plan your time and co-opt friends/family/older kids to help you manage the family/business mix.

When you have a career and a family you need to be efficient. I go to work, I get my work done, I go home. When I am at the office it's 100 per cent work, focus, efficiency and no time to waste. I deal with emails as they come up. I open all emails as they pop up and deal with them immediately. If someone emails me wanting a quick answer, it is much easier to read and send back the answer immediately, rather than leave it to deal with later. I break down emails into three categories: the ones that can be resolved with a quick answer, the ones that I am cc'd on and can be immediately deleted, and the ones that I really need some time to read, think about and respond. I like to respond and delete asap and keep my inbox tight.

Time management is also important. Do things in chunks. If I have ten minutes in between meetings or waiting for an external appointments, I catch up on emails, call my office or start writing a to-do list. If I am on a car journey, I may take a presentation with me and go through it and make my notes, so I use the journey to get work done. Or at times, on the way with my team to a meeting, I put together an agenda so we can discuss it in the car, and that saves us time in the office.

I apply the same discipline to my social life that I do to work. I get a lot of invitations to attend work, school and red-carpet events alike. I could be out every night if I wanted but I honestly don't want that and seriously I can't ... I would rather be home with the boys after work than go out. It is OK to say no to invitations. You have to ask yourself: what will I get out of being there? Is this important for my family, business or career? Who is there that I want to see? If there is no real reason for going out, don't. You have other priorities.

I have to admit that in the business/family mix there is precious little time for a real social life. You might see friends every now and again or do something spontaneous once in a while but, really, it's going to be a squeeze. You can have a career and social life or you can have a career and a family, but I don't think you can have a career *and* a family *and* a social life. You just have to pick two and go with it. That is, if you want to do the two well.

My children know about these priorities, too. They know I won't drop them off at school every morning or pick them up every day. But I will be there when they need me.

As an entrepreneur everyone wants a piece of you. Your staff, your customers, your suppliers, your family. There are times when it feels like there are not enough hours in the day to get everything done. Time is your enemy. You always seem to be running out of time and you are faced with problems coming from all different directions. Take care, you are reaching a point that can feel overwhelming ... as if you are ready to explode. Your stress levels rise, which can lead to mental or physical breakdown. You start feeling unwell, your skin and hair look bad, you may gain weight as you resort to comfort food and drink; these things are nothing but a quick fix, they will momentarily give you a boost but they don't help you to feel good in the long run.

Self-care is so important at times like this. How can you get it all done without having a meltdown? When your life

115

becomes all about prioritising others, you need to find those moments to connect with yourself, reset and rebalance. You need the time to centre yourself. You need to find a mechanism to rebalance. Find a way to mindfully focus on what you are doing in that moment and stop worrying about what is going to happen in the future. Dealing with stress is a very personal thing and it can only happen if you are committed to making changes that will make you uncomfortable.

It's difficult to take time for self-care when you are constantly bombarded by demands from work, family, friends and everything in between, but it is very important to create some space in your life. Ideally, you need to disconnect from the whirlwind around you and find a moment to be yourself every day. But how can you do this?

Make Your Needs a Priority

It can be difficult to say 'no', especially to your loved ones. But saying 'yes' all the time can make you feel depleted and resentful. Setting boundaries is crucial to allow you time to make sure your needs are met before you try to support others. Whatever your work or family situation, I am a big believer in making your needs a priority. Lead the best life that you can and use your time wisely. Imagine if someone asked you to give them £500 with no return. Would you do it? Then why are you giving them your time for free? Time is money and you have to value your time as much as you value money.

When your time is limited, you really need to choose your 'yes' and 'no's. And you have to start saying more 'no's.

A lot of us are naturally people pleasers and find it hard to say 'no' to things. When a friend asks for a favour, we tend to say 'yes', rather than disappoint. And that takes away from your work or family time, or time that you need to spend with yourself. Or we may spend so much time and energy worrying about what excuse to come up with that we end up being resentful. Part of it is not wanting to feel guilty after rejecting a friend's request, or make them feel bad or suddenly be disliked. Rather than disappoint them, we'd much rather say 'yes' and be liked. So what happens when you say 'no' and you disappoint someone? Well, you may lose some friends along the way, especially if you've always been a 'yes' person and suddenly you say 'no'. How do you say 'no' without feeling guilty?

- Buy time: you don't need to answer immediately. You can say, 'I will think about it', 'Can I check with someone first?' or 'I don't think I can make it, can I confirm with you in a few days?' Especially with the latter, you are already setting the tone that it's probably going to be a 'no' and preparing them for when the 'no' comes.
- Do you really want to do this? Be honest with yourself about whether being part of this occasion will make you happy or be helpful to you in any way. Will saying 'yes' contribute to your fulfilment? If the answer is 'no', then you shouldn't commit to it. There are of course times when you have to say 'yes' to support a loved one and you end up doing something you are not excited about, but you need to be very clear about why you said 'yes': the relationship must be very important to you. If you are saying 'yes' to someone less important out of guilt and obligation, drop it.

117

- Be honest and kind: yes, you are going to disappoint someone but it's better to be straight up. You can say something along the lines of 'I have a lot going on at work and life right now and promised myself to go out less', or 'Work is hectic right now and time doesn't allow me to take time out for a lunch.' You don't need to be specific about details: be brief and to the point. I find that the more information given as an excuse, the less genuine it looks, so stick to a simple answer. You will still not avoid disappointment and you can't control the other person's reaction, but you can control how you feel when you deliver that 'no'.

Schedule Self-Care into your Calendar

Schedule time with yourself and book it into your calendar. Anything from a mani/pedicure session, a massage, a walk in the park, a bubble bath, anything where you can be with yourself without having to manage or cater for anyone else but yourself. Slot it into your diary and let everyone know about it so you are not disturbed. It could be one hour a week, half an hour a day, whatever you can fit into your schedule. But be strict about it. You've read my morning routine in the previous chapter: that's my personal time. I take the time before the kids wake up to do the things that inspire me. Since everyone is asleep, I know no one will be around to interrupt me. Every night I go to bed excited about waking up the next morning and using that extra time, and I love planning what I can do with it. It's 5am right now when I am writing this chapter. I woke up with lots of ideas and excited about writing.

118

Tech Detox

This is a bit of a cliché but I need to address it. I don't have any fixed rules about a rigid tech detox but I know when I need to be switched on and I know when to recognise signals that I've had enough and need a break. I just go with the flow. I don't think that I have ever decided to stop looking at my emails but I know when to respond to them. There are days when exciting things are happening and I can be on my phone all night responding to emails from all over the world, or when a quick response from me at 10pm will allow a chain of actions to happen more quickly, especially when I'm dealing with different time zones. But there are also days when all sorts of challenging news arrives by email after-hours and I just think to myself, *Park this aside and deal with this first thing in the morning.* So it's not really a tech detox but managing when to deal with information that comes my way 24/7. You need to plan your own internal rules for your own lifestyle needs and wants. My way isn't necessarily the right way, but it is at least a way.

Once in a while, try a social media detox, too. I am not talking about a week of tech detox – who can do that? We are constantly bombarded with information, through email, news sites, social media. After a packed day at work, I have no space to absorb any further social media information. I don't even need to make an effort: there comes a point at the end of the day when I can't really process any more new info. From time to time, I may give Instagram a miss for a day or two ... I am sure everyone will manage to survive without a @MrsRodial post for a few days. When do you do this? Trust your gut. When new info comes up and you just can't absorb it or you feel you have started

119

to lose your Insta-curiosity, the time has come. There are times when I am craving new info, I want to get all the news I can, I want to get inspired, learn new things, see new stuff. These are the times when I know I am open to and hungry for the relentlessness of social media. If I am not feeling it, I just take a break and naturally go on a detox. Just don't force anything and if it doesn't make you happy or inspire you, it's time to take a break.

Take a Break

Sometimes all you want to do is quit. It may be too much at work, the responsibilities are piling up and you see no way out. Even in the best job, whether you work for someone else or you work for yourself, there will be times when you feel as if the only way to go is to quit. I say take a break instead. No matter how much you believe you have the perfect job, when it's all too much, just take a break. It's what I do and it's what I believe has kept me motivated and in the game for so long. For me it could be a walk around the block to grab a coffee from a new coffee shop, or leaving the office altogether and visiting some of our stores. Yes, I know, that's still work but it gives me a different energy and gets me to focus on something else. A change is as good as a rest, as they say. Sometimes I'll take a weekend away somewhere or plan a week off. To be honest, I am not a big holiday person and rarely take more than a week off, but I do realise that taking a break is really important to help recharge the batteries, get re-energised and get inspired again.

Avoid Negative People

When you are trying to find time for yourself, avoid negative people around you. There are people who thrive on negativity; it could be a friend, relative or someone in your circle who seems to always see the dark side of things and somehow, even if they don't know they are doing it, will drag you down and suck the positivity and optimism right from your bones. These energy vampires have an 'everything sucks' attitude that, if you let it, will drag you into their dark sphere, and that suits them as they hate to be sat in their negativity alone. It can start with the smallest thing: it could be a negative text or call, or a negative comment about someone who is doing great things, and you are sucked into a 'what's the point?' mindset. Try to recognise these people and avoid too much contact until you have built up your resilience, especially at times when you need to care for yourself. Surround yourself with positive people or even just be by yourself, but if you really can't avoid those negative people and find yourself in a downward-spiralling conversation, don't go along with their negativity, stay upbeat, dazzle them with light. If you are not open to them, it's more difficult for the bad vibes to break through.

Make it Happen Secret #7

10 Tips for Managing Career and Family

1. Your iPhone is your PA. Book everything as if it was an appointment. I have all my work meetings, school events, doctor's appointments and pick-up times booked in.
2. Embrace online grocery shopping. These services deliver out-of-hours and on weekends so you never have to set foot in a supermarket again. I do a weekly shopping list and have everything delivered.
3. Prioritise. Your lists are probably endless and it can be frustrating not to be able to cross items off as quickly as you want. Create two lists, one for the urgent to-dos and another with the long-term to-dos. Tackle the urgent list first and move items from one to the other as the list goes down.
4. Shortcuts are everything: anything that makes your life easier and saves time is worth it. From frozen vegetables and fruit in the freezer to an occasional Deliveroo meal: you don't always have to go for the perfect home-cooked meal every single day. Catch up on your sleep. If you don't get much sleep during the week, try to have some afternoon naps during the weekend. Every little helps.
5. Plan, plan and plan: use the weekend to plan and visualise the week, from work and family commitments to gym class and travel. Discuss these with your partner and make a plan of action of who

is doing what. Look at the seven-day period . . . take it a week at a time.

6. Accept that there will always be ups and downs. Even the perfectly arranged childcare plans can fall apart at any point. You are not alone. It happens to everyone.

7. Take a break. When it all gets too much to handle, it's OK to take a break. Take a 20-minute hot bath, go for a brisk walk, listen to your favourite podcast. Find your own way to have a short escape.

8. Find a support group of parents who are at the same stage as you; this could be a community group or a virtual online group. There are a lot of people out there who are going through the same struggles: connect with them and you can empower each other.

9. Create a world for yourself that sits outside being a parent. As small as it is, whether it is work, a hobby, a personal interest, etc., it is important to keep your identity as a person.

10. Be kind to yourself. Perfect parents and perfect situations don't exist. You are different, you are doing things your own way and you are doing your best. That's all that matters.

8

Dress to
Impress.
Repeat

As my business grew and my name was getting out there (well, let's be honest, I was putting it out there!), I started getting a lot of cool fashion party invites. One invite led to the next and soon my mantelpiece was groaning under the weight of embossed 'stiffies' for the likes of *Glamour* Women of the Year awards, *Bazaar* Fashion Icons Party in New York and the British Fashion Awards to name a few. I have to admit, it was a thrill every time a new one plopped onto my doormat or pinged to my email. I have always loved a dress-up event so it was an absolute dream to be planning my outfits weeks in advance, having my hair and makeup professionally done and living the celebrity life for a few hours. Rolling up to the red carpet, being waved through security, posing at the step-and-repeat board for a fusillade of strobing flashguns ... I have to tell you, it is as fun as it looks! And it didn't end there. The next day my picture would often end up in the roll-call of best looks from the night. And that was pretty much the form for a while: I went to a party, I got photographed, I was on a best-dressed list. The dream was being lived. I never considered it could go any other way ... but oh, I was wrong, so very, very wrong.

December 2016. A normal day at Maison Mrs Rodial ... until I started dancing around the kitchen as I had just opened an invite for one of the parties of the season. It was only the annual Stella McCartney Christmas party at her London store. Whoop! It is one of *the* most coveted events of the season, so I was buzzing. Every December, the store is decorated with the most exquisite Christmas ornaments and lights, and Stella herself hosts the party for friends of the brand. I absolutely love Stella's designs and over the years I have bought many items from her collections, from bags to dresses to jumpsuits. I'm a Stella fan! So to get this very first invite to her event was a real headspin.

The outfit planning was going to be epic ... I wanted it to be just right. Should I or should I not wear Stella? If not, who and what? There was a lot of research, a lot of calling in favours and a lot of detective work, but finally I settled on and managed to track down a stunning mesh Margiela top that I thought was ideal. It was cool and festive at the same time and was sold out everywhere. Now, it was a bit see-through ... OK, it was a lot see-through, but hey, this is fashion, and we are all adults here. Besides, I had sourced a perfectly seamless flesh-coloured bra to wear underneath it. I was a shoo-in for the best-dressed lists for this one.

I arrived at the store and it was packed. Stella was there with her team and I walked over to her to say hello and thank her for having me at her event. A photographer jumped in and asked to take our photo together. Stella was nice and graceful and full of smiles. I was feeling very smug.

Next morning, I go to my office and my PR comes in, 'Maria, you know the Stella party last night? Well, there is a story on you in this newspaper ... and it's also all over the internet.'

That's perfect ... that's exactly what we want, isn't it? I look at her face ... it doesn't quite match the news I was expecting to hear about me being on a best-dressed list. She doesn't look happy: she looks serious.

'I hope you won't be too upset, but ...' She trails off and hands me the paper.

'Stella outshone at her own party by beauty mogul pal's mesh top and nude bra combo' screamed the headline over a picture of the two of us. And that wasn't the worst of it. I was apparently wearing it to 'give the illusion of being naked' ... all the usual tabloid nonsense. I wanted to die. Here I am with one of the coolest designers in the world and I was made to look like a fool, and what's worse the papers were making out I made her look a fool! OMG, what would she think of me? Did I look cheap? Did I look like I really wanted to upstage Stella? I was mortified. People started calling and emailing about this article, I wanted to hide. I know they say that even bad press is good press but I really wanted to disappear from the face of the earth. More websites picked it up and the story rumbled on for the entire week. All I could do was just let it die down. Publicity is a double-edged sword and when it's good it's great, but when it's bad it's really bad and you just can't do anything to control it.

'The apparel oft proclaims the man' as Polonius states in *Hamlet*, or, as more regularly heard these days, Mark Twain's version: 'Clothes make the man'. It's a saying that holds true, although Mark Twain added 'naked people have little or no influence on society'. I wonder what he'd have thought of the Kim K internet-busting belfies? Or my mesh top? Anyhow, the point is that first impressions count. Clothes say a lot about you before you even say a word. Whether you have your own business, work from home, work in an office or online, the way you present yourself communicates a lot about you, your attitude and your place in society. Like it or not, clothes express who we are ... so learn to use them as part of your vision for success. As they say, 'Dress for the life you want, not the one you have.'

When I started Rodial, I was working from home. Going from working in an office (my days in banking) to working from home took a lot of adjustment. Working in an office is so much easier: you have your routine, you arrive at a certain time, you leave at a certain time and you dress in a certain way. I had an elaborate office wardrobe consisting mainly of trouser suits, black pumps and black structured handbags. I was working in a conservative corporate finance environment where I had daily meetings with clients and the image that I needed to project was of someone who knew their shit and was professional ... and my corporate-approved wardrobe did just that.

However, when I started working from home, it took me a while to figure out how to present myself. I was in a 'hands to the pump, sleeves rolled up' mindset. A 'lots to do, no time to waste on choosing blouses' kind of world. I was wearing my old sweatpants and out-of-shape T-shirt (and no, not the cool Balenciaga ones that are on trend right now, but old husband tees with stretched-out neck hole), and I'd team this with no makeup and my hair up in a messy bun. I had so much to do, I needed to be comfortable, right? I wasn't meeting anyone and my only interaction was with the Amazon delivery man.

But then, after a while, I realised something didn't feel right. Taking care of how I looked wasn't just about how other people perceived me. It was how I felt about myself. I wanted to feel in control, organised and driven, and my look had to reflect that. So I started changing things. I put together a 'work at home wardrobe' with stretchy black pants and some beautiful tops, still comfy but also neat, purposeful and stylish ... how a beauty entrepreneur should be. My hair would always be clean and neat and I would spend ten minutes doing my makeup, nothing crazy, but enough to feel good and feel like I had direction. The whole thing, from wake-up to getting into my home office, would take just 20 minutes, but it made a huge difference to how I felt and behaved. I looked successful and I felt successful.

The way I looked put me in the right 'make it happen' mindset. I was sending a positive message to myself, a message of success, and that was because I took control of my look. Simple but so effective. It also helped me set the boundaries between work and home. If I was in a work mode, I was in a work mode, full stop. My look reflected that.

130

When I finished work, I changed into my comfortable house clothes and knew my work day had ended.

It's not just how you dress, it's how you present yourself that should be very important to you. Just because you work from home or you don't have a customer-facing job, you may think that it's OK to skip the makeup or the hair and not take the time to care for your appearance ... it's just time wasted, you're getting more done. I get it, we are all busy with jobs, family, lots of responsibilities, and we may need to have one of those days, but to be successful you need to know that taking care of how you look is a big part of creating your own path to success. This is not just because you want people to see you in a certain way but because of the way it affects your subconscious mind. You should aim to be in a state of mind that is organised, and makes you feel good about yourself. If you think you look like a hot mess, guess what, you are! Whatever you think about yourself, you will be that. If you embody the mentality of not caring about what you look like, you will feel that way. And if you want to be a leader, it's even more important. Who wants to follow someone who doesn't look the part? No one. People are looking to follow someone who has success nailed down. This is why you need to put yourself together well and dress appropriately. Not because you want to impress the world, but because you need to get your mind right ... do that and the world will be impressed anyway.

Dressing for a life that you want isn't just about putting on new clothes. It's about internalising your goals and dreams. By internalising something, you absolutely believe in it and pursue it relentlessly ... and I believe that it all starts and ends with how you project yourself through the way you look.

The way you dress, talk and behave needs to be aligned with your aspirations. In order to make it happen, you need

131

to have the whole package. How you live, how you act and how you dress are important, as success requires that everything that you do is consistent with your aspirations and your goals. You need to eat, sleep and breathe it. When you dress for the life you want, you embody everything about where you want to be and where your dreams can take you. You own it. Instead of just dreaming about who you want to be, you start the day already looking the part: it stops being a dream and starts feeling like destiny. When you behave as if you already have that job/career/life, it's not just a want, it's a belief.

It's worth taking some time to really think about how you present yourself and how you are perceived by others. If you saw yourself, would you believe in you?

These days, even when I work out, I make an effort. I put on an outfit that makes me feel and look good, make sure my bun is neat and put some mascara and lipstick on, throw on my cool jacket and current sneakers. Why? Because if I feel good about myself, I will work out harder. If I look in the mirror and don't like what I see, I'm not going to be in a good mood ... and I need to be in a good mood when I am working out. I need to feel good about myself, that drives me on and makes me believe I can do better, I can do anything. I have yet to find a scenario when *not* feeling good about yourself is any benefit. I am aware that this belief may be controversial. Judge all you want. I fix my hair and wear lipstick (sometimes I even wear an undereye concealer). So what? Do what you need to do to feel better.

So, let us assume you are giving me the benefit of the doubt and fancy trying my look-good plan to make it happen, how do you get organised? I recommend having a few outfits that you can always fall back on, finding a way to style your hair that looks decent and taking no more than ten minutes to do your makeup. You are putting in an effort but not overdoing it, it's just enough of a self-care regime to encourage the right frame of mind for success. If you do see someone, it looks like you care, and if you don't, you are not going to feel it was all a waste of time and effort. The main idea is that *you* feel good about yourself and, if you care about your appearance, you will care about your work.

Now, if you know me, you know that I love fashion. While I have my uniform, I do like to keep things current and fresh when it comes to dressing. But I quickly realised I had to go through a process of change to get the balance right. I couldn't do things the way I had always done. Basically I went from being a clothes hoarder to a fashion minimalist in just a few years. Far too often, I was having that moment when you open your closet and it is so full of clothes you feel like you have nothing to wear. It happens to all of us, right?

In my early twenties I was into trends and would buy it cheap but pile it high! Bohemian chic? I was the first in line for that hippy skirt. Eighties revival? Get me those shoulder pads pronto! Seventies bell bottoms? Put me down for those! My wardrobe was a crazy mismatch of styles, colours and items that had nothing to do with each other. But what was worse, I was buying all these clothes for a lifestyle that I didn't have: endless evening and red-carpet dresses fit for a Hollywood star, an extensive summer collection of bikinis, kaftans and an impressive collection of bejewelled slides, the sort of look that might suit a woman of leisure with a villa in St-Tropez, but not north London in October. Not to mention the bags ... oh, the bags. My bag collection towered above all other items: one false move and the whole thing would come crashing down in an avalanche of tassels, quilted leather and chain-straps. The cat had a couple of close shaves while I was scaling the bag mountain looking for a particular clutch and accidently dislodged a

133

Birkin. I had every bag I had ever purchased since I was 18 (so a few years' worth ... just a few). I started to wonder whether I'd be found dead one morning under an avalanche of gold buckles and hand-crafted leather. Something had to change.

So one day, I decided I needed to edit, sell, recycle and donate. Clean up and make space for clothes that I could actually wear every day. My life wasn't red-carpet events and summer holidays. I spent most of my time in an office, at meetings or attending work-related events, so my wardrobe needed to reflect this ratio.

So began the cull. The first thing I had to do was remove myself emotionally from all those things and think, *If I was at a store today, would I buy this?* If the answer was no, or even maybe, it was a goner. Next, I'd take a good look at every item that had made the cut and, even if I liked it, if it was past its prime it had to go. If a tee was worn out, a bag looked worse for wear or a pair of favourite shoes had had their day, then it was *adios*.

That pretty much wiped off 75 per cent of my wardrobe. I started manically taking pictures and listing my designer pieces on Vestiaire Collective and eBay and anything non-branded would go to my local charity shop. Once all the old stuff was gone, I had a few favourites that I loved and kept wearing year after year. A black cashmere turtleneck, the jeans with the best fit, good-quality black trousers and a few simple tops. Shoes had to be edited too as I had a lot of occasion shoes that I never wore any more. Once I got into the groove it was easy to see what was what. Even the bag mountain was reduced to a small hillock ... finding the right bag was now more Sunday stroll than Everest base camp.

I wanted to have a clean and minimal wardrobe of a few pieces that I could wear together, mix and match, to take

134

away the thinking from my everyday dressing. Colourwise it's black, white, grey and a bit of red if I need to go for colour. That's all. The process was very liberating on so many levels. I felt free from the past and ready to move into my next phase of fashion. Did I regret selling some of the pieces that have come back in fashion (and fashion always does)? Maybe a couple of times but then that's part of the cleansing process and it's OK.

So, with an empty wardrobe, where do you go next? Well, now I could start from zero and really define how I wanted to look. My life can be crazy and may take me from a meeting at the office to store visits to speaking at a conference later on. I needed to define what my style would be and find a definition that fitted all of those scenarios. I love the idea of a core uniform, certain shapes and styles that suit me and that I wear in different variations all the time. Unlike on Instagram, where I tend to exaggerate some of my looks or show different outfits, I am much more uniform-based in my day-to-day life and 99 per cent of the time it's something black. I love a fitted, good-quality pair of trousers and an oversize top these days or, if I go fitted on the top, I need to be wearing something baggier on the bottom. If it's daytime, I live in designer sneakers, which I like to recycle every few months, and if I'm heading out to an event or appearance I'll simply add a boot or a high-heel shoe. I know it's a cliché but I love my clothes to get a lot of wear … my granny would be proud! I want clothes I can wear all the time so I need clothes I enjoy wearing. Now, I'd much rather invest in a good-quality basic that I know I will wear again and again rather than an occasion item that I will wear once.

But the real key to this type of minimal dressing is accessorising, and I love to accessorise.

Accessories are really important to my look, especially as I wear a lot of black. I love wearing a belt; they make any trouser outfit look put-together and I also use them to cinch jackets and coats for a more finished look. I don't wear any jewellery outside my wedding band and a Hermès Cape Cod watch that I have had for years.

Another thing I have been very into the last couple of years is tailoring. However, you do need to devote extra attention to making sure the clothes fit right. A well-cut and fitted jacket will always look sharp and elevate you, but one where the sleeves are too long or the shoulder, too narrow will just make you look like a sack of potatoes ... and probably feel like one too. The same goes for tailored trousers and coats: you need to ensure they are the correct length for you and your size.

When we were shooting the NIP+FAB campaign in LA with Kylie Jenner she arrived with a full-time seamstress as part of her entourage to make adjustments to the outfits and ensure they were perfect for her ... the seamstress was with us for the whole day! Was this a bit of an overkill? At most shoots you usually pin something here, tuck something there – anything for the quick fix, a bit of tape, a bulldog clip, the odd safety pin and a liberal use of the Kimble gun (the thing that fixes tags with those plastic attachments), is usually the order of the day. If you could see the reverse of most fashion shoots you'd be amazed! Anyhow, the seamstress was on Kylie's payroll, so I wasn't going to argue with that, but it did achieve a much better result: the clothes did fit perfectly! I have subsequently learned it is a thing a lot of celebs and good dressers do: they buy a suit or dress and then have it fitted by a seamstress. That's their trick.

Everyone has a different body shape and from time to time you buy something and it fits like a glove. Brilliant! However, that is not always the case so utilise the 'best-dressed' secret. Buy something inexpensive but then have

136

it altered to fit you perfectly. I guarantee it will make you look and feel like a million dollars. Something cheap but perfectly fitted beats a badly fitting designer piece any day of the week. Always go for the fit.

Coming back to the topic of being current and on trend, I know I have gone towards a minimalist and functional wardrobe but I do like to be current, and I do that by having a current detail or accessory as part of my outfit. It keeps a look fresh and is a world away from the way I would chase trends in the past. I now know what works well with my body and I stick to the shapes that work for me. I can update a basic pair of grey jeans with a cashmere top or a new pair of boots or with a cool new jacket. Jackets, however, are the thing that tends to date fastest and an old shape can make your whole look feel dated. It's now all about the oversize jackets with more laidback softer vibes so, unless it's a classic cut, I tend to have the jacket rule of one in one out, and that pretty much goes for anything 'of the moment', which means I am recycling more often. I now recycle some of the very seasonal pieces up to four times a year.

I sound like I have it all sorted, but even with an edited wardrobe and careful selection of new items, I still make mistakes and buy an ill-fitting shoe that I can't return as I've worn it already or a new tee that dates really quickly. Those items need to go sooner rather than later. No need to dwell on mistakes.

Now, while I am loving my minimal black day wardrobe, how do I dress for a special occasion? The days of buying expensive evening dresses are gone. It's just not worth it, and also the dress code for a special occasion has changed a lot. Not so long ago, no red carpet was complete without an all-out legs and boobs fest – but more recently that and the OTT bling and heels are feeling a bit outdated. Hollywood celebrities are breaking the rules by wearing unexpected outfits – there have been tuxedo pantsuits, skirts with shirts, even a black turtleneck with a statement evening skirt. Separates are the thing now but that may change even before I publish this book ... the goal is to be creative.

For separates I love to just mix and match the separates with some cool accessories. I have a fab Alexander Wang jumpsuit that had an oversize shape on top and fitted trousers – I wore that on three occasions but made it look startlingly different just by changing the belt. I added an Isabel Marant belt and grey pumps for my book signing, then paired it with a Loewe Obi belt (thanks Solange!) for the British Fashion Council/*Vogue* judging day and matched it with a Tibi white patent corset belt for a NIP+FAB launch with Mario Dedivanovic. I am now looking for the next belt to get and enjoy this jumpsuit for another year. Whatever style you find, if you want to be smart it's all about those little tweaks to update the look.

So, that's how I do it ... now, how should *you* dress for success? You want to find the style that represents the most professional image of you. When you look good, you feel good and you project the best version of yourself. So how do you find your style and keep current while still being yourself?

First and foremost, get inspired. I love nothing more than the inspiration a new season brings. This is the time when all the stores drop the new trends and clothes. Take time to go through magazines, store websites and your favourite inspirational Instagram fashion account and make a mood board. Start with things you like, then hone down to focus in on your style. Not all trends will be suitable for you, so try to pick the ones that represent your style and match your daily life scenarios ... that way you can add and adjust to suit what you already have.

My next tip would be to stick to a colour palette. The tighter the palette, the easier it is to combine pieces, but take some time to do this. It could be neutrals, black or a specific colour that you love. Whatever it is, build a wardrobe around that. It may be tempting to deviate and get that one fluorescent top that makes you happy just by looking at it, but you'll get a lot more use from a tight palette where all the colours go with each other. Be strategic when you buy new things. Think of the other pieces you already own. What can you combine this item with and on what occasions could you wear it? Ideally more than one! Don't forget to mix and match inexpensive pieces with designer, whether that's a great bag or a pair of shoes or just a belt … a designer touch can elevate a basic outfit. Just make sure that you will use the bag and shoes often too.

If you have a big presentation or meeting coming up, stick to what you are comfortable with … and repeat. I would much rather wear an outfit that I wore in the past that makes me feel confident than experiment with a new untested look on an important day. I want to be confident and focus on what I am going to say rather than worry about my skirt not fitting well or my shoes hurting.

Make it Happen Secret #8

Top 10 Wardrobe Secrets

Your wardrobe reflects who you are. We all need to reinvent ourselves and assess our style over time. What looked great five years ago may not look that great any more. Does your image reflect how you look today and who you want to be? Dress for the job you want, not the job you have, as they say. But seriously, looking good and projecting the best possible image combined with your own personal branding can take you places.

1. Declutter, declutter, declutter. I used to review my wardrobe one or two times a year, and I would still keep a few things for sentimental reasons, hoping one day I would wear them again. Over the past year I have been ruthless. I have gone down to bare bones and have only kept pieces that make me feel good while wearing them. I now have less but when I open my closet I like what I see and I wear it all.

2. Don't save pieces for special occasions. I don't shop for special occasions any more and if I spend money on something I need to make sure it takes me from the office to a cocktail. I always think twice before I buy something and, whatever it is, it has to pass the adaptability test and go with at least another two or three pieces I already own. This way I enjoy everything I buy rather than saving it and possibly never wearing it.

3. Go for separates rather than dresses. I used to buy a lot of dresses that proved to be difficult to mix and match, and I would end up only getting a few wears out of them. Now I invest in skirts and trousers and can dress them up or down with a tee or a blouse, or I put the jacket with jeans, and create many more looks.

4. Update your look with shoes. I find that the trends in clothes don't change as much as shoes. I do like to wear the latest shoe but equally I don't keep old pairs. I'd much rather they find another home through Vestiaire Collective or eBay. I give away my high-street pieces to my local charity shop. Remember the rule: one in, one out.

5. Day bags have a bit more longevity. I like a big, luxurious day bag in black that I can use *every* single day for at least a year. It needs to fit everything for my day but also needs to travel and hold an iPad. I like to invest in a designer day bag from Balenciaga or Givenchy as I use it a lot and it's worth the investment.

6. I'm not bothered so much about investing in a load of evening bags as I think they are overpriced and I don't really care about making a statement with an evening bag. I buy a good-quality simple clutch from Celine or Off-White in black/white – my criterion is always that it goes with everything and I can use it all the time.

7. Tailoring is important. I almost always have to tailor my trousers and jackets to my height. The fit has to be right for a pulled-together look. Tailoring can also give an old item a new lease of life, something

141

I have done recently with some old trousers ... it's amazing what a little tailoring update can do.

8. I use a lot of belts to pull coats or jackets together at the waist or on trousers and jeans to give them some interesting detail.

9. I never invest in summer clothes. I have a wardrobe of simple tees and shorts, and may get an occasional new pair of sandals, but it's a wardrobe that's not really important to me, especially as I live in London and I'm working most of the year. I'd much rather invest in winter clothes and all-weather basics.

10. Jean shapes change with fashion and can look very outdated very quickly. I have started investing in just one or two pairs in dark grey, black or white. I find these colourways far more sophisticated than standard blue denim, especially the light washes that can look unprofessional. I love a good old worn-in pair of Levi's though: they have great shape and quality.

Make it Happen Secret #9

10 Tips for Travelling in Style

I can't talk about dressing for success without talking about travel. It's important to look well put together when you fly. Why? Well, again, it's about feeling great about yourself but also you never know who you may bump into. I have made some of the best business and personal connections on a plane and you want to give your best impression at all times.

Travel is a big part of my life. From a day trip to visit a new store in Europe to a week-long book tour in the US or a press event in Hong Kong, I am always on the go. Over the years I have picked up some travel tips to make the best out of my trips, disrupt my life as little as possible and look great while doing it! These are my learnings:

1. Make your trip as short as it needs to be and not a day longer. I like to be efficient when I travel, meaning if I can do it all in a day trip, I will wake up at 3am, take a 5am flight, do my meeting and be back home the same evening. All that checking in the night before, packing and unpacking, checking out the next morning takes time, is expensive and adds complexity that I don't need for a quick trip. Yes, I have to wake up earlier and I have discovered that coffee is my best friend at these times ... but I'd much rather not check luggage. I simply arrive with my handbag and can be back home pronto ... probably before some

people on my flight have even left the baggage carousel. It saves me time away from my family and work that I cannot afford.

2. Being in the beauty business, I always take my own beauty products. Where do we even start? Skincare, masks, makeup, hair products. I even want to take my own shower gel, shampoo and body cream as I can't really bear the hotel amenities ... even when they have pretty good brands. I am here to tell you that these so-called brand products have been de-spec-ed down to a basic formula, so you aren't really washing your hair in £100 shampoo, it's like a basic version. However, this isn't true for the travel-size products you can buy in the shops: they are generally the same standard. Another time saver here is to have two sets of wash bags. One set I use at home and I have the exact same set of products always ready to travel. They stay in the wash bag and I just replace them when I run out but I never unpack them. This saves me about an hour of thinking about what I need, and means I never forget a cleanser, a mask or a hairbrush.

3. Get that healthy glow. Travel can take a toll on your skin and lack of sleep can make you feel and look tired. I always apply fake tan when I get ready to go on a flight, and have some Rodial Dragon's Blood Eye Masks ready to go. I wear loose clothes and by the time I arrive I am relaxed and have the perfect tan – one that lasts me for a week.

4. Work out what suits you best in order to deal with jet lag. I am still looking for the perfect formula for

the jet lag I suffer, especially when I travel to the US or Asia. I'm in NY all the time and the first night I usually wake at 3am, and half an hour later every day. If I am there for a week, I ultimately get there and fully adjust. If I am there for a couple of days, I kind of give up and keep London time, meaning I am in bed at 7pm and up at 3am. I get the day started with calls and emails from the UK office and then get on with my day in NY. I sleep on the flight back and have no jet lag when back home. There is no point in trying to fight a 3am wake-up and forcing myself to sleep. This gives me more anxiety and I end up just tossing and turning for a couple of hours before I properly wake up again. Instead, I order a bowl of berries, hot water and a double espresso at 3am and get the day started with a bang!

5. Travel in style, in terms of luggage. For my main suitcase (which become suitcases during Fashion Week) I like a good-quality but not expensive nylon roller bag with an expandable zip. I like my luggage to look good, but it doesn't have to be designer as it's thrown left, right and centre between flights and I would worry if I spent too much money on it. I replace it every three years when it's worn or things start falling apart. I like it black as it always looks great and I get a cute name tag from somewhere more elevated, so it has a personal touch and makes it easy to recognise when a ton of black nylon bags come out of the conveyor belt. Now, my carry-on luggage is another story. I used to have a little black Muji carry-on to take my essentials

145

(iPad, magazines, books, beauty-on-flight products, chargers, etc.) but one day I was passing by the Louis Vuitton store at Heathrow Terminal 5 and got drawn to a carry-on with the grey and black Damier style. This is a men's pattern but I find it a lot more sophisticated and less obvious than the classic brown LV print. It was simply gorgeous. The material, the silver of the zipper, the quality of the finish. My birthday was around the corner and I decided to treat myself to it. Sometimes we spend on things that we use or wear once or even not at all. I travel all the time and I can have a piece of luxury with me every single time. And it was duty free, which saved me that tax, which is always a bonus. I love this bag so much, it fits everything I need and gives me a little bit of happiness every time I travel. The next year at my birthday, I got the matching wallet and now I am good with luggage for a while!

6. Keep warm at all times. Even if I travel to a warm destination, I find that I always get cold before or during a flight. It was summer and I was in NY on a business trip. On my way back the flight was delayed by five hours and I was stuck at the airport in my summer gear. The aircon was blasting and I was wearing a short-sleeved T-shirt, with no jacket or anything else for cover. This was when I decided to always bring with me a generous black scarf. I read in interviews that many frequent travellers take a cashmere blanket every time they travel. I couldn't do that. First of all, I don't have space for a blanket and, also, I tend to leave things behind. Seriously,

I can't even tell you the amount of blankets and scarves I have left behind on the airlines of the world. So I get a generous scarf. It might be a light wool or cashmere mix in the winter or soft cotton mix in the summer, and this I can use to put around my neck or use as a blanket. I keep it in my carry-on and it's always ready to face the elements!

7. Bring some snacks with you. Sometimes food is available on a flight, sometimes you have a choice, sometimes you don't and all you get is a dry sandwich with a ton of bread and butter and very little else. If I have a bit of time to plan, I bring a bag of cashew nuts and some green tea bags to ensure I have my own snacks at all times. When you are hungry, you will eat what is available and, if you are following a healthy diet, it's just not worth breaking a healthy nutrition plan for some bad-quality food. Planning is everything!

8. Use your flight time creatively. Every flight is different, my mood is different and I take the opportunity to do something different. There are times when I travel at the end of the week and I am exhausted, and all I want to do is binge-watch a Netflix boxset that I downloaded on my iPad. There are other times when I need to be online and if it's a work day and I happen to be travelling with American Airlines, I take full advantage of the in-flight wifi and it's business as usual. I accept that it can be a bit frustrating at times when everyone tries to get on the wifi at the same time and your connection drops just at the moment you are awaiting a crucial email response. At other times,

I buy all the new fashion and business magazines and all I want to do is read and cut out pages for my inspo folder, and then there are the odd times when all I want to do is sleep through the flight and completely switch off the world. This is the only time when no one can get hold of me (if I don't log on to that wifi or let my team know it's available!). Use the time during a flight as your personal time to do whatever feels right. I personally cherish this time and look forward to it.

9. Think about your airport look. Have you heard that celebrities have a specific stylist that puts their airport look together? When you see pictures of X/Y/Z celebrity looking immaculate in the latest jeans and boots, perfect hair and subtle makeup and those oversize sunglasses, they didn't just happen to wake up and throw any old thing on. Airport looks are part of a celebrity's portfolio of pictures and they need to look as good in the airport lobby as they do when they are on the red carpet. That is, put together, on trend, but looking like they haven't tried that hard. I don't have any paparazzi waiting me at the airport (thank God, I have enough going on without worrying about professional hair and makeup on the way to the airport!) but I still want to look well put together, relaxed and cool when I travel. All black with an interesting jacket and a fashion sneaker, that's my look. I like to keep it with stretchy fabrics and simple fitted lines and I will throw on a designer jacket by Balenciaga or Off-White and a new-style elevated sneaker, and I'm good to go. Hair and makeup should be minimum

148

effort. I like to pull my hair back in a bun. It's easy to do, looks sophisticated and it takes a few seconds. I don't like to wear a lot of makeup when I fly as want my skin to breathe during a flight but I do put on some Radical skin tint and concealer, and I do a quick smoky eye, blush and lipstick and I'm good to go. I like powders in general as they make my pores disappear but never use powder on a flight. I need to let the pores breathe.

10. Get moving. When I arrive at my destination, I like to get moving. I will go for a walk around the hotel, or do some stretching in my room or go to a yoga class if it's a big city and one is available. Anything to get my body moving and unclog the muscles after hours of sitting on a plane seat. If I need to get to sleep I will eat something light before I go to bed, have a warm bath or shower and try to get as relaxed as possible to help a good night's sleep. I always pack workout gear when I travel. I don't always use it but I know it's there and at least I won't have an excuse. I am up at 3am anyway, so I may as well hit the hotel gym and get some action going before the day starts!

9

Zero Motivation? No Problem

As you may have guessed by now, my work day includes a lot of social media action. However, it's not all just selfies and seeing what the Kardashians are up to; a good chunk of my online time is spent researching new and interesting influencers/bloggers. Over the years I have discovered some amazing content out there and there is new stuff appearing every day, so it's something I really have to keep on top of ... not that it's a chore, I love it!

There was one blogger in particular I started following on Instagram, let's call her Erin, whose posts I adored. She had a blog and an Instagram account that was themed around fashion, beauty and fitness. Every weekend she posted a Q&A with a different health/fitness/fashion/beauty theme all delivered in her unique style. I really enjoyed her work, especially her stories, which like her posts were really nicely filmed and edited and very interesting and real. I was hooked. So the next time we hosted one of our regular blogger events at the Rodial counter, I obviously asked my team to invite her.

When she accepted I was very excited to meet her and we had a very nice chat (I think I just about managed to keep my super-fan excitement in control). She told me that she had a full-time job during the day and was working on her blog on the side, doing whatever she could in her spare hours in the early mornings, after work and at weekends, and she hoped that one day she would make the transition to blogging full time.

I came away really excited and inspired by her story and looking forward to seeing her next steps. After all, it sounded very familiar to a certain self-made beauty entrepreneur I knew (ahem). I followed her with even more anticipation after that and her blogs were brilliant as ever. I predicted big things. However, just a few months later she completely disappeared from my feed. Just like that, she stopped posting.

I'd only met her once but I felt like I'd lost one of my closest friends. Social media can be strange like that sometimes ... you can feel like you know the people you follow personally: you see their face, you share their highs and lows, you follow their journey. I know it's weird to admit but I got quite worried about her. Why is she not posting? Is she OK? My weekends had a huge blog-shaped hole in them now ... they would never be the same again.

A few months later I bumped into her in one of our stores and of course wanted to know what happened. I had formulated all sorts of wild kidnap/blackmail/alien-abduction scenarios so was braced for an epic tale, but it was nothing like that ... She lost her motivation one day and so decided to take some time off until her muse came back and, guess what, nine months later she found that the motivation still wasn't there. In the meantime, she had got a promotion and things were going so great at her day job that she decided to drop her blogging side-hustle. Although her promotion was great, I was devastated for her, she had been my inspiration and I was so looking forward to seeing her build her personal brand and influencer direction but that sudden loss of motivation along the way was something she just didn't come back from. I mean, don't get me wrong, she seemed perfectly happy in life and with her new job, but all I could think of was where would she be with her blog if she had persevered?

In the months that followed this episode I thought a lot about the power of self-motivation. She had started strong, kept it going for a bit and then ... boom! Now, I don't know the personal circumstances surrounding her decision, so of course there may have been more to it, but whatever happened, she lost her motivation and it happens to all of us.

So, you are in the right mindset, your goals are set and you have your plan of action. You're ready to get out there and make it happen for yourself, but then you have a few setbacks, and suddenly things aren't going as planned. You don't want to quit but you are just not feeling it. You wake up one day and you have zero motivation. People around you are letting you down, you've had a bad day, things are taking much longer than you hoped. Everyone around you is going at a slow pace, you feel like everyone else needs an intravenous drip of double espresso to get them going. You feel like you are going for it at 200 miles an hour but the results are rolling in as slow as a tortoise ... a very old tortoise. Pushing against this wave of difficulties, you start to feel a little ground down. Naturally, you think to yourself, *I am not feeling motivated, let me take a few days off my plan and wait for motivation to come back to me.*

Stop (or rather, don't stop). Just don't do it. You can't take a break from motivating yourself. Know that there will be days when you are ready to take the world by storm and days when you aren't. The key to success is to keep on going and keep motivating yourself whether you are feeling it or not. The key to success is consistency and doing something *every single day* to take you closer to your goal, whether you're feeling it or not, and take it from someone who has been there, there are lots of things that can make you feel like throwing in the towel. So what are some of the things to look out for that can crush your motivation?

Too Much Information

When you are conducting your research into your goals you will naturally get exposed to an overload of information. You need to focus. If your goal is to lose weight and you look up ten different diets, you can't start the Paleo Diet

155

one week, go vegan the next and the following week switch to the California Cookie Diet, you'll just be overwhelmed, and you'll probably have put on weight. Just focus on one. Too much information can take your motivation away and paralyse you. But 'info in' is only one half of the story; 'info out' is also something to consider. Let's say you are a blogger and you have worked on your strategy but still it ends up all over the place. One day you do beauty, then fashion, then lifestyle, then cooking. Yes, it's true that in your mind you want to be all of those things but it's just overwhelming. Focus on one thing. Do it well. If it's not working then fine, move to the next. Assess the result, give it a chance and be flexible to change but always remember how important it is to keep focused.

Comparing Yourself to Everyone Else Around You

You look at ten different people, everyone is doing their own thing and you compare yourself to not one but all of these people around you. Just stop. Right now. Take them out of your mind, your feed, your life. Comparison is the beginning of the end. You must follow your own journey. A lot of people ask me how can I be a significant part of the action these days when beauty is so saturated. And yes, I admit it is a crowded market, and not only do we compete with all the usual big beauty brands, but also with new start-ups, not to mention the seemingly endless supply of mega celebrities and influencers with millions of followers that launch their own beauty brands every day. Well, if I woke up every day analysing and worried about the competition, I would be a nervous wreck. I don't. I am aware of what they

156

do but I choose not to invite them into my day-to-day life. I am in my own lane and I do what I think is right for my business and my customer. I am not ignoring the competition but I am not obsessing over them either.

Lack of Consistency

If you want to make it happen, everything should revolve around you and your goal. You need to keep the motivation going, whether you're feeling it or not. You need planning and dedication even when you are fully fired-up, and at the times when you are at a low ebb this will prove invaluable.

Let's say you want to build your own brand while working full-time somewhere else. Think of the possible obstacles and how to overcome them. What time do you need to get up? How many hours can you put aside to work on your side-hustle? How are you going to find that extra time? How about cutting down the time you are spending on social media or watching boxsets, and put this time and effort into building your brand? Be prepared to work hard and know that there will be sacrifices.

As you have already seen, I had to sacrifice my social life to get where I am. I am up between 5 and 6am in the morning to work on my goals, write my book, prepare for my podcasts, make plans for my business. That means that I need to be in bed by 10pm each night and after a full day's work at the office I just don't have time for a social life or at least the kind of life I used to have. But I'm OK with it. It's become more important for me to work hard on my goals rather than be tripping around dinner parties, theatres and cocktail bars, and to top it all I also do some work on most weekends. But I'm not being a martyr. In fact,

I don't see this as a sacrifice at all. Working on my goals and knowing I am building something make me happy. These are not sacrifices, they are choices. If you apply the same planning to your play time as your work time then you will find that you can achieve a good work/life balance – after all, I'm not trying to make you into a robot!

I have learned that in order to keep your motivation going, you need to feed it constantly: read books, research articles, listen to podcasts. Even a few minutes a day of reading or listening to a motivational piece will help you. You don't have time? Get an audio book, listen to a podcast on your commute or as you drive or do the housework. (Check out my *Overnight Success* podcast... it is the perfect accompaniment to doing the vacuuming!) But whenever or however you do it, do try to read or listen to something motivational *every* single day. That means on the days that you feel motivated as well as the days that you don't. After all, even if you feel great about your motivation levels, you can always feel better, right? You will never say, 'I have too much motivation, if I go on like this I may explode.' I haven't seen anyone suffering from a motivation overdose, so keep on feeding your brain with motivation, even if you are on top of your game. Feed your mind with positive messages. Brainwash yourself in a positive way.

Interaction with Negative People

As mentioned earlier, having negative people around you can very quickly sap your motivation to zero. I'm sure you can pick out the odd toxic person in your life. I certainly can, and we all have them. I am a half-full glass person but do have to deal with a lot of glass half-empty people out there.

I used to be really affected by other people's energy but lately I have started following some new strategies in order protect mine. Put simply, you may not be able to change people but you can change the way you react to them. The way that I do it is first of all prepare myself mentally for interacting with them. I may meditate for a few minutes, keep a smile on my face at all times, do whatever I can to not bring myself down. And then I immediately plan something that would raise my vibe again. It could be taking a walk and getting some fresh air, going to a nice coffee shop or cool restaurant and ordering myself a nice cup of coffee or a little treat, and surrounding myself with high-energy positive vibes. I also love visiting my teams at the stores so I'll see my best sales people and talk about products, sales and customer feedback, and, if I have time, I'll sit down and have a mini makeover.

I'm talking here about protecting myself from people I know will bring me down, but even if you can't prepare when you meet a vibe-vampire for the first time, you can still use the 'post-downer' strategy I describe here. Anything it takes to raise your vibe and take yourself away from a difficult or toxic conversation. It only takes me five to ten minutes of a positive high-vibe interaction to get over a negative one. Give it a try! Once you get back to your positive mental attitude, you can get your motivation back on track. You'll be unstoppable!

At certain times, all of the above challenges will assail you; at others, only one or two, but let's assume for the sake of this lesson on motivation that everything else around you is positive and you know what you want to achieve, but you are starting to feel that the task is just too big and you can't find that essential motivation. What is the one thing to do when your motivation level is at zero?

The first thing to do is to break it down. Let's say that you want to exercise. You have woken up, you were planning to go to a morning class but just can't get your head around it today. You start thinking up seemingly rational excuses: I don't feel like it, I won't be able to follow the class, I don't feel like I have energy, it's cold out there, what difference would it make anyway, I'm out of shape, one class won't change anything, etc, etc., ad infinitum. Before you know it you've missed a month of classes. What you need to do is break down your resistance step by step. Let's take the early morning gym class as an example:

1. Step 1: I don't have the energy: have an espresso, instant fix.
2. Step 2: It won't make any difference, I'm out of shape: stop thinking negatively and just put on your workout clothes. Wear your nicest workout clothes and sneakers or invest in some. You want to feel extra good about yourself.
3. Step 3: It's cold out there, I'd much rather stay home: put on a warm jacket and download your favourite podcast or playlist, and get out the door. You are warm and entertained on your way to the gym. Or if everything else fails, call an Uber. Just find a way to *make it there.*
4. Step 4: Everyone else is fitter than me. Look around you. Does it look like everyone else is in better shape than you? Chances are a couple of people may be but most of them are just like you and it may be their first class too. You have nothing to fear.
5. Step 5: I won't be able to follow the class: you're in the class. The instructor is now in control. It's their job to help you. Relax and enjoy it.

160

6. Step 6: The class is hard, you want to quit. Don't. Just keep on going. Adjust the class and pace yourself so you can finish it. Lower the weights or the number of repetitions. Give it enough energy but don't go so hard at the beginning that you have to leave early. Do the best that you can so you can finish the class. Work smart.

As a different example, let's imagine you want to work on a presentation but can't get it started:

1. Step 1: Make your working area as inviting as possible. Tidy up the clutter, burn a candle, get some flowers in a vase.
2. Step 2: Turn on your computer and open the program you will use, but shut down your other notifications (email, etc.) as they will distract you.
3. Step 3: Give yourself a time frame: make a deal with yourself that you'll work for the next 30 minutes non-stop without any interruptions.
4. Step 4: Write the title of your presentation.
5. Step 5: Start writing all your thoughts about this project as they come into your mind, in no particular order.
6. Step 6: After 30 minutes save your work and shut your computer down.
7. Step 7: Go back at it the next day with a fresh mind. Add more ideas for another 30 minutes.
8. Step 8: Keep on doing this for a few days until you have some material and go back at the end of the week and edit and put some structure to it. Your presentation will be done in no time! If you don't have days then simply compress the time – take an

hour's break then come back to it, review the next morning and so on to fit your timescale or deadline.

The general rule for overcoming a lack of motivation is to 'Just Take Action'. It's the law of attraction. When you take action and project positive vibes out there, action will come back to you. The law of attraction isn't just about visualising where you want to be and then sitting there and waiting for the universe to make it happen. It's about visualising while at the same time sending those positive vibes out to the universe with your work and energy. You are creating a chain reaction, and even a very small movement counts as action. Just do something. Send an email, have a conversation, write down your goals, make that phone call. Just do something every single day that will take you closer to your goal. Be positive and the law of attraction will bring it back to you tenfold.

Now, sometimes there is a big project that we want to start but we never really seem to find the time. It could be anything: starting a business or a new hobby, reorganising our closet or home to clear space and open ourselves to something new, doing the accounts, taking a class, clearing our inbox, booking holidays or learning a new skill. These are all things I have done and all of them required me to take a deep breath before I dived in. But once I was in I was glad … the water was lovely!

The biggest and deepest breath I have taken recently was completing my *Overnight Success* podcast project. I recorded a few episodes and felt it was heading in a good direction but everything was still up in the air. I needed to write the intros and outros to add to my recordings, write and record a trailer, decide on a day and time for the launch, etc., which sounds simple – make a list, break it down, right? But when I did the hole just went deeper; the more I looked into the task the more there was to do. To do the intros and trailers I had to listen to the existing recordings, make edits, summarise each one, find the highlights, make sure they had a narrative feel and get it all to tie together. This was a big project that needed not only a lot of time but also my full focus and attention. It wasn't something I could fit into half an hour here between accounting meetings and store visits. I needed clarity, I needed time and I needed to be 100 per cent focused on this. But I could not fit it in during my day. And so I kept on delaying it. Major procrastination territory.

So I slotted into my schedule something I have subsequently decided to call a 'Mega Make It Happen Day': a full day when I could focus on just tackling this massive project. This would be a Sunday as this is the day that I have the least going on at work or in life. It's a day that usually is without interruptions or disruptions and it helps that I get some rest on a Saturday so I am generally full of energy on a Sunday. I got prepared in advance, bringing everything I needed with me. My phone was off (and I promised myself no social media for the day). I got all my paperwork, files and recording devices at the ready, I got my hot water with lemon and my favourite espresso, lit my favourite candle and had some extra notebooks and coloured pencils to make notes.

It was exactly what was needed. This was one of the most productive days ever. With this pre-planned environment giving me clarity of mind, I managed to record all the material I needed, wrote down the content and even emailed it all over to my team for the next steps. All I could think about on that day was Project Podcast. No other work, no meetings, no social media distractions, just that one goal. And I have to say that without that day, I seriously doubt I would have launched my podcast.

Sometimes making a start is hard. We tend to procrastinate when faced with what seems like a big challenge and delay getting started. So, if you have a big project that you've been delaying then organise a Mega Make It Happen Day. Rather than taking small bites of time every day, put aside one full day, either a day off from work or on a weekend. Whenever you decide, book it ahead of time in your diary and get ready for it.

Make it Happen Secret #10

10 Steps for a Mega Make it Happen Day

I want to share with you my top ten steps so that *you* can plan your Mega Make It Happen Day:

1. Tell your family/roommate/cat that you'll take the day to complete your project and that you don't want to be interrupted. Don't be afraid to say no if anyone tries to interrupt and you can be honest to them about the reason.
2. Have your space decluttered the day before, have a candle ready and some fresh flowers. Create the most inviting, clean and luxurious space so you can enjoy your work.
3. Write your to-do list for the day and tick off as you complete the tasks. Keep beautiful pads and coloured pencils around and your mood board/ research close at hand, ready to keep inspiring you.
4. Get rid of any distractions, put your phone on silent and don't be tempted to get on it to check social media and new updates.
5. Decide how many hours you will be working on this project and stick to it.
6. Start your day a bit earlier than usual, so if you usually start work at 9am get it started at 7am. By 9am you'll already feel you are ahead of the game.
7. Have your favourite drinks around you to keep hydrated and energised and stop regularly for meal

breaks. You don't want to be running on empty and deplete your energy.

8. Background music is always great, but I recommend starting in the quiet to get some progress and focus, then use music to lift you when you really need it.

9. Reward yourself when you finish your day with something that you like: have a long gossip/chat with a friend, take a long bubble bath or watch your favourite boxset. You need some passive entertainment to clear your mind.

10. You've had a Mega Make It Happen Day, well done! Plan your next one already and slot it into your diary.

Ready to Make it Happen? Let's Do It!

About a year ago, I was invited to give a talk at British *Vogue*. They invited over 150 guests to attend an exclusive Q&A with *Vogue* Beauty Editor Jessica Diner and myself at Vogue House in London. This was a big deal, after years of appearing at smaller events and building up to bigger conferences (including *WWD*), gradually increasing my confidence in my public speaking, I had finally got the golden ticket. Speaking at *Vogue*! I couldn't have been more excited, this was a dream come true! The magazine that I had idolised for years had *me* as a guest speaker.

This was a special day and I prepared as much as I could. I carefully studied the questions and rehearsed my answers so I was ready for the night. I booked professional hair and makeup so I would look immaculate for the pictures, and I had a brand new Balenciaga outfit and shoes to make me feel like a million-dollar boss babe. All had been planned to perfection. My team arrived at the venue a couple of hours ahead of me to set up and I was going to arrive a bit later. My talk was starting at 7pm. I planned to arrive around 6pm to check out the space, connect with Jessica Diner and the *Vogue* team and get ready for my talk.

At 5.30pm, hair and makeup on point, I get into the beautiful Mercedes that had been hired me for that evening, ready to be driven to *Vogue*. Travel time between my home and *Vogue* was usually between 15 and 30 minutes depending on traffic so I am bang on schedule, maybe even a little ahead. I get into the car and am on such a high, I can't wait! Fifteen minutes into the journey, it looks like there is a bit of traffic. *That's usual for this time in central London, not to worry,* I think, *I said I'd be there at six, so we have another 15 minutes built in.* I call my team as I wait and they tell me that the guests are already queueing outside Vogue House, but I'm still sitting in traffic. I want to be there to see it ... people queuing to see me ... how exciting! I am afraid that I am one of those people who thinks no one is ever going to show up to anything I do, even though I know the tickets sold out an hour after being posted on the *Vogue* website. I still worry about those things.

Another 15 minutes pass ... it is now 6pm and I am still in the car. I ask the driver if he has a guesstimate of our arrival time. His reply hits me like a ton of bricks. It seems that they have closed the whole of Regent Street in the rush hour to start putting up the Christmas lights. If you know London, you know that Regent Street is always busy so closing it has caused a gridlock for 20 blocks in every direction and Vogue House in Hanover Square is slap bang in the middle of it all. The driver points out that we are only two blocks away, so did I want to go out and walk? In my five-inch Balenciagas? You must be joking! Plus, I want to arrive in style, it's only just gone 6 ... if I arrive at 6.30 that's still OK. I'll stay in the car, we'll follow the diversion and it'll all be fine.

Another 15 minutes later we are still crawling through the maze of side streets behind Regent Street and I am starting to really worry now. Is that Berkeley Square ... what are we doing here? This diversion is taking us to the other side of town.

My team is calling, *Vogue* is worried, people are waiting, where was I? Looking at my watch, it is now 6.40.

168

'When do you need to be at your event?' the driver asks. 'Well, half an hour ago ideally,' I say, 'but I'll settle for 7pm.'

He doesn't crack a smile. Oh dear. His honest assessment is that we may be in the car for another two hours. I am stunned into silence as he turns to me, and with a sigh says, 'So if you want to make it, I would walk if I were you.'

I am now officially panicking. There is obviously no other way. I get out of the car, it's dark and I have no idea where I am. Just to put it in perspective, I have no sense of direction, never have. I get lost coming back from the bathroom most days. I can't read a map to save my life and I don't actually know London that well (even though I have lived here for ever). I have been dropped somewhere off Oxford Street, which *is* a main road, but I think I am at the opposite end to Vogue House. To be fair, even if it is the right end, you might as well have dropped me off in Downtown Dubai: I would still have no idea how to get to *Vogue*.

I call my assistant, and she begins trying to guide me through the maze like a manic game of blind man's bluff.

'Where are you? What can you see?'

'There's a Starbucks on my left and a McDonald's on my right...' Again, I might as well be in Dubai as there are about eight branches of Starbucks on Oxford Street. This is not working. I am wandering around like a lost kid.

Finally, I decide to get over my map phobia and follow my phone navigation. I start walking, phone outstretched, Balenciaga outfit swishing, heels clicking, making my way through the bemused tourists and work-weary Londoners when I suddenly reach a part of Oxford Street that I recognise... yes, I know where I am... I suddenly get a sense of calm. What's the time – 6.50? I can do this. I message my assistant: you'd better have a stiff drink waiting for me when I arrive as this has been a hell ride!

She WhatsApps me a picture of a glass of champagne ... that gives me the boost I need! I am in pain walking in my Balenciaga heels but I'm visualising the moment I would be in Vogue House sipping that chilled champagne and that keeps me going.

At 6.57pm, three minutes before my talk is due to start, I make it to Vogue House. My feet are in pain, my makeup is melting and my hair isn't looking great either. I go to the ladies to powder up and pull myself together. This whole ordeal hasn't seemed real. It's been like an out-of-body experience. The glass of champagne barely touches the sides. I do a quick body-scan meditation, take a few deep breaths and think to myself, *All of these people are here for you. They've paid for an expensive ticket, they made their way here from all over the city and the country and you have a responsibility to give them what they are here for. There are no excuses, pull yourself together and make it happen.* With that thought, a weird sense of energy shoots through me and gets me on a high, so by the time the host announces my name, I stride into that room with huge self-confidence and deliver one of my best speeches ever.

That evening could have evolved in a number of different ways. I could have refused to get out of the car and ended up an hour late for my speech. Most of the people would have left, or been really disappointed or upset. I could have played the diva card, decided it was too stressful and cancelled (I would never have done that, but many do!), or I could have arrived miserable, complaining, blaming everyone and everything for my woes, and taken that negativity into my speech and out on my audience. All of these are scenarios that have transpired with celebrity speakers at events. I've been in the audience for a few and I have heard the stories from others I know in the industry. I could have gone down one of those routes, but I didn't.

Why? Because I was really looking forward to connecting with all the people that had made the effort to get tickets to come and see me, and every single one of them motivated me to try to do an amazing job. I owed it to them and I owed it to myself and my brand to be the best, in whatever the circumstances. We all feed off other people's energy and when I see a group of gorgeous 'make it happen' boss babes ready to be inspired, I get all the motivation I need to make it happen too. The feeling that I knew I would get when I finished my speech and the anticipation of connecting with all those people gave me what I needed to keep me positive and keep me marching down Oxford Street in those heels ... and that glass of champagne wasn't bad either. At that specific moment in time, this was my motivation and my motivation helped me make it happen.

This is very much how life and business works. You may have it all planned out but, believe me, challenges come to us every single day. It doesn't matter at what stage you are at in your life or your career, nothing is smooth sailing. In fact, there is a quote by Franklin D Roosevelt that goes, 'A smooth sea never made a skilled sailor', and it's true, we learn best from life's challenges and to face them we need a daily dose of motivation. Every time you have a setback, you need to go back to your motivation. It will get you through the hardest days: it's like magic. Your success comes from following through on your plans whatever it takes. You will have your good days and your bad days. You may love what you do but you won't love every day of it. So be ready. Don't get disappointed. Don't give up.

We are all different and have different goals and dreams but the process to achieving them is always the same. Find your motivation, take action, keep your inspiration going, power through the challenges, bounce back from rejection, have a laser-like focus and keep going even when you don't feel like it.

We all know there are no shortcuts to success. You need to put in the work, you need to put in the hours. People come to me and say, 'I am frustrated as I haven't reached my goals yet', and when I ask them how long they have been doing this, most of them answer under a year, even just six months. Success takes time, it could be two years, five years, ten years or, as in my case, even eighteen. Don't expect too much too soon.

And don't settle. When you achieve one goal, set the next one. Aim high. Dream big. Whatever stage of life you are at, there is always another goal, there is always another dream you can aim for. Most importantly, enjoy the process. Have fun while you're hustling. It can seem hard when you are going through it but with time and a little perspective you'll look back at your challenges and recalling how you overcame them will put a smile on your face ... and there might even be a book in it!

Be grateful for everything you have achieved. It's easy to focus on the things you don't have but, remember, it all starts with being grateful, thankful and proud of what you have achieved so far. Cultivate the positive, grateful mindset and the energy that will attract more positivity. Don't forget the law of attraction: what you project, you will get back.

Keep on learning. I've learned more by reading, listening to podcasts, attending conferences and being around successful people than I learned at school. If you surround yourself with success, you *will* be successful too.

You are the average of the five people you hang out with the most, so I repeat, surround yourself with success. Choose your circles carefully. Be around positive and successful people to elevate yourself and put you in the right mindset for success, and I don't just mean the people who we surround ourselves with in the real world, but also the people we are interested in and follow on social media. Follow successful people and people who inspire you, the ones that project positive vibes of success, the kind of success that will rub off on you too. For a start, you can give me a follow @MrsRodial on Instagram (another shameless plug here I know, sorry). But seriously, just try to eliminate any negativity, people or situations that sap your positive energy; find the people and inspirations that will bring more positivity and success in your real and digital life.

Above all, believe in yourself. Have a clear vision of where you want to be and don't stop until you get there. Just keep going. You *will* make it happen!

Love,
Xmaria

Acknowledgements

I'd like to thank my editor at Ebury, Carey Smith, for believing in my second book even before I wrote it. This is proof that there IS overnight success, after you've proven yourself the first time. I am grateful to have found Rory Scarfe as my agent. He's been the best at sharing my vision, helping me keep my cool and leading me to the right decisions. A huge thank you to Sean Cunning for helping me to edit the book and for teaching me to keep things light and not take myself seriously. My illustrator Emma Kenny for drawing the most fabulous illustration for my book cover and for bearing with me with those 1am emails when I would wake up panicked about whether we should go with the Givenchy or the Celine handbag. We got there in the end. Finally I'd love to thank my team at Rodial for always supporting me on my projects, and my fabulous @MrsRodial Instagram & Overnight Success podcast community, you all inspire me more than you would ever know.

INDEX

178